Travels wit

Travels with a Laptop

Michael Hewitt

INTERNATIONAL THOMSON COMPUTER PRESS

I ⓣ P   An International Thomson Publishing Company

London • Bonn • Boston • Johannesburg • Madrid • Melbourne • Mexico City • New York • Paris
Singapore • Tokyo • Toronto • Albany, NY • Belmont, CA • Cincinnati, OH • Detroit, MI

Travels with a Laptop

Copyright © 1996 Michael Hewitt

I ⓣ P A division of International Thomson Publishing Inc.
The ITP logo is a trademark under licence

British Library Cataloguing-in-Publication Data
A catalogue record for this book is available from the British Library

Library of Congress Cataloging-in-Publication Data
A catalog record for this book is available from the Library of Congress

First printed 1995

Commissioning Editor: Liz Israel Oppedijk

Typeset in the UK by Keyword Publishing Services, Barking
Printed in the UK Clays Ltd, St Ives plc

ISBN 1-85032-164-7

International Thomson Computer Press
Berkshire House
High Holborn
London WC1V 7AA
UK

International Thomson Computer Press
20 Park Plaza
14th Floor
Boston MA 02116
USA

`http://www.thomson.com/itcp.html`

Imprints of International Thomson Publishing

Contents

vi Contents

Foreword

In the three years that TeleAdapt has been in business we have dealt with many professionals who carry a laptop on their travels, but I must admit that when I first spoke with Mike Hewitt about connecting a laptop to the telephone system in Cuba I thought we must be dealing with MI5 or the CIA! Fortunately he carried on to tell me that he was a freelance writer, and was interested in writing about TeleAdapt, finding out whether we really could meet his demands, and testing our claim to be able to get him connected in a country that we would consider decidedly challenging!

Mike did go to Cuba as you will read in the pages to come, communicated successfully from there, and thus established himself in the top ranks of the laptop cognoscenti of the late 80s and early 90s who had realised that there was more to explore in a hotel room than the contents of the minibar. Indeed, in the late 1980s there suddenly appeared around the world a new breed of traveller—those who on a long distance flight would find themselves staring at a smaller screen than the movie variety; those who paced the aircraft searching in vain for power sockets to charge their dying batteries, and those whose first inclination on arriving in a hotel room was not to try the softness of the bed or the efficiency of the shower but instead to seek out the elusive telephone socket to plug in their modem! Yes, in the 1980s the 'road warrior' or more appropriately the 'road worrier' had arrived. This is the business traveller, equipped with a laptop, who needs to communicate with company or clients by fax and email, and more recently to 'surf' the Internet. Thus TeleAdapt was born to help these 'road worriers' overcome the problems of using a fax/modem in a strange land by adapting their phone jacks to those of the country being visited, and to provide solutions and support for connecting to any type of phone system world-wide, 24 hours a day.

In flying terms, Mike always seems to be 'pushing the envelope'—going that bit further in the pursuit of a story. In a Cuban hotel or a helicopter over Blackpool he wants to prove that it can be done. Fortunately for us at TeleAdapt, Mike's modem connectivity demands are not typical of the majority of our customers who tend to beat a more sedate path around the business capitals and business hotels of the world, allowing us to provide a more uniform service. However, if there is a new mobile communications opportunity, a new laptop/phone system angle to be found, I think we can be pretty sure that Mike will be there before the majority of us even think about it, blazing a trail for others to follow.

Good reading: *Travels with a Laptop* offers excellent stories and tips for the most seasoned 'road warrior' as well as the most inexperienced 'road worrier'. And for both, we at TeleAdapt are pleased to be associated with Mike and of service to the laptop traveller.

Gordon Brown
Managing Director/President
TeleAdapt UK, US, Australia

31 August 1995

Argentina
TDPT 261D

Argentina (2)
TDPT 262 S

Australia
TDPT 011 D

Austria
TDPT 021 D

Belgium
TDPT 031 D

Brazil
TDPT 201 D

Colombia & Venezuela
TDPT 241 S

Czech & Slovak Reps
TDPT 041 D

Denmark & Portugal
TDPT 051 D

Finland & Norway
TDPT 061 D

Scandi (New)
TDPT 062 D

France
TDPT 071 D

Germany (New) TAE F
TDPT 081 D

Germany (Old) ADOS4
TDPT 082 S

Germany East
TDPT 084 S

Germany ADOS8
TDPT 086 S

Germany VDO4
TDPT 080 S

Greece
TDPT 251 D

Holland
TDPT 121 D

Hungary
TDPT 091 D

India (UK Old)
TDPT 271 S

Israel
TDPT 221 D

Israel (Old) Greece
TDPT 222 D

Italy
TDPT 101 D

Italy (Old)
TDPT 103 S

Middle East
TDPT 291 S

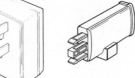

Jordan, SaudiKuwait,
M.east
TDPT 281 S

Japan
TDPT 111 S

Korea, Saudi Arabia
TDPT 191 S

Poland & Russia
TDPT 131 D

South Africa
TDPT 141 D

Sweden
TDPT 151 D

Swiss (New)
TDPT 161 D

Swiss (Old)
TDPT 162 D

Turkey
TDPT 211 D

UK
TDPT 174 D

USA
TDPT 179 D

Yugoslavia (Former)
TDPT 181 D

TeleDaptors
courtesy of TeleAdapt Ltd.
(Tel. +44(0)181 421 4444)
S = Simplex, D = Duplex

Introduction

Whys and Wherefores

Very simply, this book is about traveling away from home with a portable computer and using it to keep in touch. Its intended readership could be business people, on the road sales reps, jet-setting pop stars, journalists, or even globetrotting tourists sending a letter home. Indeed, anyone who owns a portable computer and modem combination will hopefully find it useful.

That said, some might ask why, as we approach the twenty-first century, such a book is necessary. Haven't all potential communications difficulties now been overcome, thanks to orbiting satellites and vandal-proof telephone boxes? The answer is unclear: they have and they haven't. But let's first take a look at what the situation used to be, and take it from there. If nothing else, it will at least show how far we've come.

The Moving Target

Contacting a business person on the move, especially if they were traveling abroad, used to be rather like trying to hit one of those plastic ducks at a fairground rifle range. In the pre-air-travel age, for example, letters from Head Office to the over-seas employees had to go by packet steamer. Assuming they actually made it to dry land (bear in mind the 'R.M.S' in R.M.S Titanic stood for 'Royal Mail Ship') there was then the ordeal of an overland journey, by train, stagecoach, or rickshaw.

Even with fair winds, friendly natives, and bunion-free feet, the time-lag between dispatch and arrival could be weeks, if not months. After such a hiatus, there was no guarantee that the intended recipient would still be around. For their part, the employee could never be entirely sure that Head Office was still solvent. So it became a matter of necessity to devise faster, more efficient means of keeping in touch.

All long-range communication methods had their problems: pigeon post could end up re-routed into a pie; the electronic telegraph was susceptible to woodpeckers on the pole; the first international telephone calls took hours to set up, were extremely expensive and the connections none too clear or long-lasting. It's only comparatively recently that, thanks to satellite and digital technology, long-distance international calls have become truly reliable.

However, as any parent of teenagers will confirm, sending voice messages by telephone isn't in fact a very cost-effective means of communicating, particularly internationally. Consider how much, say, a 30 minute transatlantic call costs, and ask yourself how much useful information you can convey in that time.

The spoken word is actually a very inefficient communications medium compared to the printed variety. As an example, a single page of a broadsheet newspaper, which can usually be read in five to ten minutes, carries as much, if not more, information than a whole 30 minute news broadcast.

Bitmap Transmission

It was perhaps this realization that led the international business community to embrace, first, the telex, and latterly, facsimile communication – the fax – so wholeheartedly. Now, at the push of a button, letters, memos, company reports, and the like can be turned into bitmap images (like newspaper or television pictures) and shifted from any fax-equipped site in the world to any other in just minutes. Imagine how long it would take (and how much it would cost) to read the equivalent amount of information over the phone.

But even the proven fax has its drawbacks. For a start, it's a station to station system. While this might not be much of a consideration with national calls, international calls can soon crank up the bill. Although you might not be using the telephone line for very long (typically, a single A4 page of 300 words takes between 30 seconds and a minute to get to the other end) you're still incurring long-distance charges while you do.

Aside from this, there could be other potentially inconvenient variables to consider. If your contacts are constantly on the move, how do you guarantee your fax will reach them? Are they certain to be in the same hotel every night? Indeed, are they even staying in a hotel? Can you be sure that the hotel has a working fax machine? Do the staff keep a regular check on their fax in-tray? Can you be sure they'll deliver it to the right room? Then again, would you want a hotel employee to see what could be a highly confidential company memo?

This brings us to the successor to the telex and fax, and the system that's set to transform business, and indeed domestic communications, totally: the so-called 'Information Superhighway.'

Digital Data

There's still a lot of confusion as to what this 'Information Superhighway' actually is (mainly fostered by trendy media types who don't know what the hell they're talking about). In fact, as it stands, there's nothing 'super' about it. The term refers simply to a globe-straddling web of largely bog-standard computer networks, linked by dedicated landlines and conventional phone lines. But the long and short of it is, a message sent from any one computer in that network can be transmitted to any other in just seconds, with almost complete confidentiality.

So How Does it Work and What are the Practical Advantages?

Suppose you want to send a letter from your PC in the London office to your colleague's PC in an equivalent office in downtown Sydney. What happens is that, initially, the PCs in England and Australia exchange data, not directly with each other, but with intermediary computers based, typically, somewhere on the outskirts of each of the two cities. These in turn automatically relay the information over dedicated landlines to a string of intermediate servers scattered throughout the Far East and Europe. It's the daisy chain or 'pass the beanbag' principle.

As a result, it becomes possible for a PC in the UK to send an electronic message to a PC in Australia simply by contacting the London server. For its part, the Antipodean PC downloads that message by phoning Sydney. Each computer operator pays only for the cost of a local call, plus the network charges, the two of which add up to far less than a station to station international phone call.

The Mobile Office

Of course, it needn't simply be office-bound PCs dialing into that network; anyone traveling with a modem-equipped portable computer can just as easily connect. So, with no difficulty at all, business travelers are able to jet from country to country, computer in hand, log on wherever they happen to land, and download and transmit all their messages in seconds. With the push of a few buttons, the office effectively becomes wherever the traveler happens to be at the time – a hotel, a private room, or even a telephone box.

Actually, most of that last paragraph is a load of nonsense. If it were that simple, you wouldn't be reading this book, and I certainly wouldn't be writing it. So let's cut the crap, as they say, and get to the nitty gritty.

The Unpalatable Truth

Fact: traveling with a portable computer is rarely hassle-free. For a start, you're subject to routine X-ray and security examinations, weight restrictions, and the machinations of baggage handlers. Your computer can be impounded by customs, stolen by opportunistic thieves, have its data erased by magnetic fields, or even explode when connected to a dodgy transformer. And if it survives the journey, you've then got to face the problems of communicating the fruits of your on-the-road labors back home.

Yes, connecting to a foreign telephone network, and thence to the Internet or a commercial service such as CompuServe or America Online, *can* sometimes be a simple push-button operation. People are actively working towards making it so. For the moment, however, it usually isn't. Not only might the traveler have to cope with noisy international lines and their vagaries, they may also have to contend with prehistoric exchanges, antique telephones, unrecognizable dial tones, and a collection of incompatible phone sockets whose number and variety would put H. J. Heinz to shame. That's if they're lucky and can actually find a socket willing to accommodate the plug.

But Who is this International Traveler?

I'm assuming there are two types of people who regularly travel and communicate using a laptop. The first, and by far the minority, will be those who are completely at ease with technology. They know which aircraft seat is closest to the power supply for recharging their portable's batteries. They probably use online services, such as CompuServe or Prodigy, on a daily basis. Terms such as 'modem initialization string' and 'V42 error correction' trip off their tongues as easily as 'A large   scotch and soda, please.' If they have a problem, they're usually sufficiently self-reliant to sort it out for themselves.

Then there's the second category – probably the majority of us. We're not even sure that the airline will allow us to carry our computer onboard. We're worried Customs may confiscate it at the other end. And above all, we're probably technophobes. After the Dark Ages of DOS and the Command Line Interface, we've now become spoilt by user-friendly front-ends like Windows or Macintosh. In our offices, everything is point and click. This goes for sending faxes and downloading e-mail, too. So when we're out on the road with our portable computers, we expect it to be just the same. We want to simply locate the phone socket, plug in, and click on 'Send,' as we do back home.

If you recognize yourself in that description, then this book is above all for you.

Travels with a Laptop

As far as is possible, this has been written as a non-technical book. Where there is jargon, I've attempted to explain it as fully as possible without sounding too much like an editorial from *Batteries and Wireless Weekly*. In carrying out the research, I've drawn on my own experiences and those of other travelers. Much of the expertise we've gained is largely down to shared knowledge which, through this tome, I now hope to share a little more widely.

And who exactly am I? Just a wandering freelance journalist with an interest in hi-tech and gadgetry who, by necessity, has had to become proficient in laptop usage and international telecommunications. But don't let that put you off. I imagine we all have one thing in common, regardless of our individual occupations. We're busy people who need to get on with our jobs, and part of that job involves working away from home with a portable computer.

That said, the first chapter deals with portable computers in general, the question of which one to choose, and the necessary peripherals, such as extra batteries and modems. If you haven't already purchased a machine, I'll examine the options available, based on the sort of work you need to do. For example, someone who merely has to send e-mail on an irregular basis might be very well served by a simple palmtop computer. On the other hand, a person who has to process accounts on the road, program elaborate spreadsheet, or edit complex graphics files will probably require a sophisticated, high-speed notebook.

Then I'll look at the practical aspects of traveling with a portable computer. Is it really feasible to use one while traveling Economy? What sort of restrictions do airlines impose and why? What are the options if your batteries suddenly go flat? How are Customs and Excise likely to react to the sight of a brand new laptop? And of course you can't talk about traveling these days without mentioning airport security and its attendant hazards, such as X-rays or overly zealous staff. Where there are likely to be problems, I'll highlight them.

Chapters 3–5, the most overtly and unashamedly technical, deal with what to do on the ground at your destination. Specifically, how do you contact home using your portable computer? Here, I examine the mysteries of telephone plug adapters, acoustic couplers, hard-wiring, cellular modems, and satellite links. Don't worry – although it's not exactly a non-trivial procedure, connecting through a foreign telephone system isn't as vastly complicated as many so-called 'comms experts' would have us believe. Believe me: if a freelance journalist can do it, anyone can.

Finally, there's no point writing a book about international computer communications unless you talk about some of the commercial service providers, such as CompuServe, America Online and, more generally, the Internet. So Chapter 7 takes a look at a number of the high-profile conferencing and information systems, and highlights the services they offer, in particular those, like e-mail and online travel agencies, that are likely to be of most use to the business traveler.

So there we are. I trust that within these pages I'm able to cover most of the problems that the international telecommuter is likely to face. Inevitably, however, somewhere in the world there's going to be some weird telephone setup or bureaucratic red tape that no one's yet come across. If you come across such a case and survive the experience, I'd be grateful to hear from you. Then I can incorporate your problems and – hopefully – their solution in a subsequent revision.

Bon voyage.

Mike Hewitt

1: Which Computer?

If you already have a portable computer, modem and other peripherals, you may prefer to skip this chapter. If not, it could help you make up your mind which type to buy, but it isn't by any means an exhaustive model by model review. If it were, this book would be out of date before it left the printer, given the rate at which technology is forever advancing. Besides, different models and (especially) their peripherals can sometimes be specific to certain countries.

Rather, then, I'm looking at the varieties of portable machines on offer and trying to assess which might best suit your individual needs, whether you're a roving business person, a journalist or simply a tourist. This isn't to say I won't home in on particular pieces of hardware and give a brief description and assessment, but where I do, it's usually because those machines best exemplify the sort of functionality you ought to be looking for.

Anyway, onwards.

Basic Requirements

Question: what does a traveler, any sort of traveler, really require from a portable computer – apart, of course, from its being truly portable?

Everyone's basic needs are probably much the same, whoever he or she may be: a useable keyboard, a legible screen, a means of storing the input data securely over long periods and, perhaps most important, staying power. In other words, the batteries should last at least as long as a flight, subsonic, across the Atlantic.

After that, though, the waters become murkier.

Just as there's no such beast as a universal DIY appliance, in the same way there is no portable computer that will suit the needs of everyone. This is because different jobs require different tools. If all I want to do, for example, is store address and telephone information, then a Pentium-based **laptop** with an integral **VGA** color screen and digital sound is most probably overkill. On the other hand, trying to make a sales presentation on a 4 inch **palmtop** might exhaust the patience, and eyesight, of all but the most understanding clients.

To date, portable computers break down into three types. In descending order of compactness, they are: personal digital organizers (that's 'palmtops' to you and me), **sub-notebooks** and **notebooks**. These last two are commonly referred to as 'laptops.' Of course, the pedantically inclined may pull me up on this and point out that, strictly speaking, the official designation of a laptop is a computer with a clamshell case that weighs more than 6 pounds. Ignore them. I'll use it (as does the majority of the computer-literate population) as a generic term for any portable above palmtop size.

Incidentally, you'll perhaps have noticed that I'm ignoring **penpad** computers – those that rely on inbuilt **handwriting recognition** or store their input as **electronic ink**. This is because, at the moment, so is everyone else. There's a niche market, albeit a very limited one, for such machines as the Apple Newton and the Casio Zoomer. Unfortunately, though they're nice executive toys, the technology hasn't yet matured for them to be taken seriously as business tools. Put bluntly: they can't read handwriting particularly efficiently. Maybe in another ten years.

So having narrowed the field, which is for you?

Palmtops: The Limitations

Technically speaking, nowadays there's no reason why, like James Bond's Q, manufacturers can't shrink computers to cufflink or wristwatch size. Indeed, a few do, but not with any notable commercial success. Most of the potential customers have probably been put off by the complexities of physically entering data into, say, a Cartier 486 DX or Patek Philippe Multimedia PC. Even if they manage, how do they then display what they've input?

Unless you can train a pet monkey to operate the thing on your behalf, the degree to which a computer may be miniaturized is restricted by the dimensions of the human hand and the resolving power of the human eye. The current palmtop size is therefore about as small as it's possible to get and still be useable. Then again, how useable *is* a palmtop? Can it ever take the place of a full-size machine?

Depending on your needs, and the machine, the answer is a qualified yes, but only inasmuch as a bicycle can replace a car. Sometimes it can, of course, and is often better suited to the task. Just as you wouldn't try to drive a Lamborghini down a narrow mountain track, so it's impractical to tuck a 486 laptop with a protruding tracker-ball down the front of a pair of Lycra shorts.

With this in mind, there are six basic points to consider:

1. If you're a touch-typist, you won't be – at least, not successfully – on a palmtop. The main problem is the **keyboard**. Most are lousy, being either too cramped, too unresponsive, or both. Those on a few select machines are, however, acceptable. 'Acceptable' is how a Pavarotti fan might describe Frank Sinatra. Therefore, journalists and others whose job requires a lot of heavy duty text entry would probably be best advised to look at another type of computer.

2. Maybe you're used to working with **Windows**-based programs, like word processors or spreadsheets, on the office PC. Bear in mind that palmtops can't run this sort of software. Some palmtops are DOS compatible. In other

words, they either have, or are able to emulate, the operating system used by most personal computers at work, **MS-DOS**. However, their processing power isn't nearly enough to allow them to handle any but the most basic DOS packages. By 'basic', I mean vintage WordStar and prehistoric versions of WordPerfect. Forget anything modern and Windows-compatible, such as Word or Excel.

3. Palmtop Liquid Crystal Displays (**LCDs**) are usually monochrome and, in order to conserve power, without a backlight. Because they *are* so small compared with those on laptops, they're often difficult to read. This is especially so in subdued lighting.

4. Unlike a conventional computer whose peripherals, such as printer cable, modem, serial link, and so on, are usually standard and can therefore be sourced anywhere, most palmtop peripherals tend to be non-standard and proprietary. In other words, if you buy a specific make of palmtop, you're usually forced to buy that make's printer and cables, too. And by locking you into a single source of supply like this, the manufacturers are able to, and indeed often do, charge well over the odds for their peripherals.

5. Like the peripherals, the operating systems on most palmtops are proprietary, specific to a particular brand. This brings two problems. First, unless your chosen palmtop is a popular model, third-party software houses usually won't bother writing programs for it as there's no commercial incentive. You're therefore reliant on the software provided by the palmtop's manufacturer. Second, because the software *is* specific to the machine, you can't transfer a program written for one make of palmtop to another make.

6. The current generation of palmtop computers doesn't have anything like the storage capacity of either a desktop or laptop PC. Data is usually saved to so-called 'volatile

memory.' In other words, if the batteries fail you lose all your work. Some palmtops can save their data to non-volatile storage media for extra security. But while a PC will write its files to either a standard floppy disk or an internal hard drive, palmtops have to use solid-state alternatives, mostly proprietary and – surprise, surprise – relatively expensive.

Palmtops: The Advantages

On the face of it, the above points would seem to militate against purchasing a palmtop. They need not. In fact, certain models are regarded by some people as practical alternatives not only to conventional laptop computers but also to office-bound PCs. Thousands of business people are happy to word process their important correspondence, maintain spreadsheets and databases, and even send e-mail, all using a little palmtop.

How Come?

1. Because a palmtop owes more to electronic calculator technology than to PC technology, at the moment it remains the only true 'go anywhere' computer. It's certainly the only type that's both light and small enough to fit into a jacket pocket. This means it can be taken out and fired up in seconds, ready to record any fleeting thoughts as and when they fleet. Also, palmtops are far more robust than laptop computers, and – within reason – can be dropped or sat upon with relative impunity.

2. The majority of palmtops are powered either by conventional AA, or small 'penlight' size batteries, which can be bought inexpensively virtually anywhere in the world. Because it doesn't have power-hungry extras like backlighting and disk drives to worry about, the average

palmtop's battery life is usually at least five times that of the most sophisticated laptop – enough to keep you going around the world several times, and more, without recharging.

3. Those with nimble fingers can achieve *reasonable* speeds – maybe 30 words per minute – on a palmtop. Success depends on three factors. The first, naturally, is that you have a good machine providing decent 'tactile feedback' from the keys. Second, the machine must be used on a steady, level surface. Balancing it on your lap is out. Third, you must be able to hear a keyboard click. It's no doubt psychological, but if those clicks are turned off or are drowned out by ambient noises, most users report that their typing deteriorates dramatically.

4. Although palmtops generally aren't able to run the same programs as the office PC, the inbuilt programs on some models can be very good in their own right. Also, the majority are able to exchange data with desktop PCs. So, for example, you can start work on a document using the office word processor, save it in an intermediate file format, and then transfer it across to the palmtop for further editing, and vice versa.

5. A few of the better palmtops are what are described as 'systems' machines. They're marketed together with a complete range of business software, such as accounts programs, spreadsheets, and databases, as well as all the necessary peripherals, such as fax modems, connecting cables, storage devices, and so on. The gist of it is, you can carry something which encompasses most of the functionality of a full-size office computer in either a briefcase or a couple of pockets.

6. Palmtops are relatively inexpensive. If yours is lost, stolen or damaged, your insurance company won't be as

aggrieved as they would if a similar disaster occurred to an expensive laptop.

Given all of this, how do you choose the right model?

Palmtops: Three Popular Makes

As with any type of computer, you really must try before you buy. Ideally, sit down with a knowledgeable salesman and get 'hands on' experience. If the keyboard and screen are uncomfortable to use in a showroom, for instance, they will be even more so at, say, 20 000 feet in a cramped, vibrating aeroplane. Similarly, if the salesperson can't demonstrate the palmtop in operation with a decent range of peripherals and add-on programs, the odds are they don't exist. Look at another model with better systems ability.

In the absence of such a salesperson, I'm going to stand in myself and examine briefly three palmtops. My choice isn't necessarily based on any personal preference. It's just that these models currently happen to be three of the most popular, and incorporate the sort of functionality and features you ought to be looking for in a machine of this size. That's to say, a reasonable keyboard, useable software, and good connectivity with desktop PCs, printers and online systems.

At the time of writing, the world's affections seem largely split between Personal Digital Assistants (PDAs) from Sharp, Hewlett Packard, and, increasingly, Psion.

Sharp 9000

Known in the USA as the 'Wizards,' these units all have their origins in electronic calculators. One of the top models in the range, the 9000 measures just over 6 inches long by $\frac{3}{4}$ inches wide and $\frac{7}{8}$ inches thick, and weighs a little under 11 ounces. When folded flat, it looks almost exactly like a wallet, and takes up about the same amount of space in your pocket. The unit is powered by two AAA batteries, giving an effective life of 60 hours plus.

So what are this device's virtues? In my opinion – and I must point out that others disagree strongly – the QWERTY keyboard is just about the best of any palmtop, with generously spaced keys that give a nice, responsive 'beep' when depressed. With the wind blowing in the right direction, I've been able to achieve typing speeds exceeding 35 words per minute, with surprisingly few mis-keyings. My hands aren't exactly small, either. I was trained as a compositor, and am therefore used to heavy, well-spaced typesetters' keyboards.

The second virtue is the integral **pen** (or more properly, a stylus, as there's no ink in the thing). This has a number of functions. Foremost amongst them is that it allows you to either highlight text or choose menu items simply by placing the tip on the touch-sensitive screen. This is a much faster and more efficient way of working than ploughing through layers of hierarchical menus. Or you can use the pen to draw such things as maps and diagrams directly on to the screen, and then save them as 'electronic ink'.

Being a systems machine, there's a range both of internal and add-on software and hardware. Built-in applications include a rudimentary word processor, fax software, an address book, an extremely efficient scheduling tool, and a calculator. Additional software includes a spellchecker and thesaurus, a spreadsheet, and communications packages for accessing conferencing systems and sending e-mail.

On the peripherals side, there are wireless infra-red adapters that allow data to be transferred to PCs and printers. There's also an integral infra-red receiver/transmitter that permits two Wizards to exchange data with one another. This is handy for communicating across boardroom tables or transmitting illicit pick-up lines in some of the more technologically aware singles' bars.

On the conventional communications side, Sharp's optional CE-FM4 Fax/Modem, measuring just $0.7 \times 1.7 \times 3.5$ inches, attaches neatly on to the side of the Wizard. A cable leading from this plugs directly into any phone line or, via a cellular interface, to a mobile phone. Using the Wizard's inbuilt fax software, you can create faxes with cover pages and send them directly from the palmtop, without having to print them out first. The modem can also be used in combination with the Wizard's own terminal software for accessing online services, such as CompuServe or the Internet. Unfortunately, the interface is rather, let's say, austere.

Verdict: rugged, dependable and, for a palmtop, a very good keyboard. The pen functionality is a winner, too. However, the inbuilt applications, especially the word processor and terminal software, leave something to be desired in terms of functionality and appearance.

The Psion Series 3a

About the size of a schoolchild's pencil box ($6.5 \times 3.3 \times 0.9$ inches), the 3a's grey, clamshell design opens up to reveal a surprisingly large and legible monochrome LCD screen and a QWERTY keyboard. It looks cramped, but with practice, a professional typist can achieve half-decent speeds. Two fingered 'hunt and peck' typists – the majority, according to studies – should be better served.

The great strength of the Series 3a lies in the range of programs and add-ons that are available, either from Psion themselves or third-party vendors. These include accounts packages, communications programs for different online systems, language translation software, and even maps of the London Underground. The built-in software includes a word processor which is as functional, if not more so, than many on conventional PCs. In addition there's a spreadsheet, (reminiscent of Lotus 1-2-3, one of the top desktop programs) a scientific calculator, an alarm clock, an agenda, and a database.

The Series 3a stows easily in a jacket pocket and runs off two standard AA batteries. These give it a life of, typically, 40 hours. There are connection kits allowing the 3a to transfer data to and from the office computer. It can also be connected to a pocket fax modem, the **Psion 3Fax**, to provide full Group 3 fax compatibility (albeit, because of memory constraints, without the 'receive' capability). Effectively, the Psion 3a provides similar features to a fully equipped desktop computer, albeit in pocket dimensions.

Verdict: probably the best systems machine with the best word processor of any PDA. On the downside, however, the peripherals – especially the cables for transferring data to and from other computers – tend to be (to my mind, anyway) unreasonably expensive.

Hewlett Packard HP 200LX

Boasting a battery life of 60 hours, weighing just 11 ounces and able to fit into a shirt pocket, the HP 200LX must be one of the smallest DOS compatible computers there is. However, as I mentioned before, this virtue is of dubious value given the limited processing power and memory of the machine.

That aside, the HP 200LX's inbuilt applications are extremely impressive. They include Lotus 1-2-3 (a pocket version of one of the leading desktop spreadsheet packages), Pocket Quicken (a palmtop-optimized version of Intuit's popular personal-finance package), and Lotus **cc:Mail**. This last is an e-mail management program, whose specific functions I'll come to in a later chapter.

For all this, the keyboard, unfortunately, is rather disappointing. Hewlett Packard have squeezed a numeric keypad into the bottom right-hand corner, which means there's less room for the QWERTY keys. As a result, although it's easy to enter numbers, text entry is something of a hurdle, liable to many mis-keyings. If, as we're told, everyone has a novel in him, it isn't advisable to try writing it on the HP 200LX. Not a long one, anyway.

That said, if you can get the text in, the HP 200LX probably makes it easier than most to get it out. As well as the cc:Mail, there's a resident DataComm program for connecting to other computers or online services, a variety of infra-red wireless or conventional links, a built-in serial port and an optional fax modem. Also, the HP 200LX has a **PC Card** slot.

(A *what*? Sorry. This is the new term for what used to be called – and it's a mouthful – a Personal Computer Memory Card International Association, or **PCMCIA** device. These are industry-standard, credit-card sized peripherals, such as modems, storage units, and network interfaces that can be swapped between different types of computer and used for exchanging data. You just plug in and play. More later.)

Verdict: an unimpressive keyboard lets down what would otherwise be a very impressive machine, but if you absolutely insist on MS-DOS compatibility and cc:Mail, there really isn't anything to touch it.

*　*　*

Having read this far, you may already have decided that a palmtop isn't for you. If so, what are the other options?

The Notepad – A Hybrid

There's an awful lot of snobbishness associated with laptop computers, much of it generated by the computer press. The situation is akin to the car market: if you haven't got the newest and most sophisticated, you're regarded as a wimp. But do you really need the horsepower and performance (and price tag) of a full-blown 486 laptop? Might a more basic computer suit you just as well?

We've established that, thanks to its minuscule keyboard, a palmtop isn't really appropriate for heavy-duty text entry.

Other than that, however, it would be the ideal machine for those, like roving journalists, whose prime requirements are a reliable text-entry engine and a means of getting that text back to base. If this sounds like you, then it could be worth looking at a sub-division within the portable computer world, the generic term for which is usually **notepad**.

A notepad is an A4 size machine which shares most of the characteristics of a palmtop. In other words, it has a long battery life, proprietary inbuilt software, proprietary hardware, (usually) a non-backlit LCD screen and a certain robustness. And, of course, it's relatively inexpensive. On the down side, a notepad is too big to fit into a pocket. But − and this is the major advantage − its size means that it can incorporate a standard, full-travel keyboard.

Here are some examples. Again, I'm not on commission from the manufacturers. It's simply that the machines described below have a proven track record and thousands of satisfied users.

Psion MC Word

The MC Word (launched as the MC400) is actually the A4, $4\frac{1}{2}$ pounds forerunner of the Series 3a, mentioned above. It has a full-sized, full-travel keyboard, an 8 inch monochrome screen, and a similar word processor to the palmtop 3a. If word processing is all you need (there are also basic, inbuilt calculator and address book functions, and a terminal emulator for data transmission) then this computer would certainly fit the bill. It's solid state, well-built, and gives a battery life of around 60 hours from eight AA cells. A conventional modem can be connected to the back through an optional serial cable. The MC Word is available directly from Psion.

Amstrad NC100

People − usually computer journalists − can get unnecessarily snooty about the Amstrad name. There's no need to. They produce reliable, easy-to-use machines. Indeed, Amstrad say of their NC100 Notepad, 'If you can't use this new computer in five minutes, you'll get your money back.' Weighing less than $2\frac{1}{2}$ lb, the NC100 has been designed for non computer literates who just want a basic, no frills business tool rather than something that will blind people with its sheer technical sophistication.

There are four colored buttons on the bottom left of the full-travel keyboard, corresponding to the onboard functions. When the machine is turned on, a message on the screen prompts the user for the function they require. These functions include a word processor with a 48 000 word spell-checker, an address book, calculator, calendar and diary, and world clock with alarms. There's also a facility for attaching a modem to the back of the machine.

The LCD screen displays eight lines of text, and the inbuilt word processor, Protext, is compatible with the version used on PCs. Alternatively, documents can be saved as simple text, without formatting. Data transfer between the NC100 and the office computer is remarkably easy. Simply connect a cable between the two and fire up the inbuilt comms software.

The NC100 runs from four AA cells which give a useful life of about 40 hours. Not only is it lightweight and long lasting, it can take the knocks. Even if it falls off a table, it will keep on running (don't try this too often, though). The same can't be said for many conventional laptops.

Amstrad NC200

The NC100's big brother, the A4 size NC200, is like its sibling, but sports a 16 line backlit display, an inbuilt spreadsheet and a disk drive. Although the drive takes standard $3\frac{1}{2}$ inch disks, the data isn't compatible with that in standard desktop PCs. The disks should therefore be looked upon merely as a backup storage medium, to supplement the computer's internal memory. Besides, using the drive adds somewhat to the power drain, as does the backlight. Even so, four AA cells will give you a highly respectable 20 on-the-road hours with both these features used continuously.

* * *

But perhaps your job demands a portable computer that can run the same software as the machine at the office. For example, you might be an accountant who has to maintain a complex spreadsheet, or a sales rep with a massive database full of clients and contacts. Or maybe you need to run a graphics-intensive presentation program for marketing, **DTP** or educational purposes. Or maybe you just want something to whip out in a trendy café in order to look cool. If so, you'd be well advised to consider buying a notebook or a sub-notebook computer.

Notebooks and Sub-notebooks: The Requirements

The first laptops, back in the late 1980s, were a joke. Their low-resolution LCD screens made 1930s' Baird televisions look good. They effectively redefined the concept of portable: you needed to pop steroids just to lift the things, and if the battery lasted longer than an ice-cube in a greenhouse, *The Guinness Book of Records* would send a man round. Apart from that, they were marvellous, innovatory pieces of technology – just not practical. So what do I mean by practical?

Practical means doing exactly what the office PC does, but doing it on the move. It means having a keyboard that allows touch typing without inducing repetitive strain injury, and a display that doesn't promote myopia. And it has to carry on working for a sensible number of hours between recharges. Finally, all of this practicality has to be crammed into something not much bigger than a brick layer's lunch box.

A Tall Order?

Well, consider the minimum specification for a modern office PC. Today's top business packages, such as **Word for Windows** and **Excel**, require a 'fast' processor. A 486SX is now regarded as the bare minimum. Soon, no doubt, a computer with a Pentium processor will become the entry-level machine. Office PCs also need a lot of computer memory – called **RAM** (random access memory) in technospeak – and **hard disk** space. The minimum requirements here are *at least* 4 megabytes of RAM and a hard disk of 100 megabytes. For navigation, operating pulldown menus and clicking on icons, office PCs need a mouse. And, of course, for data entry, they need a full-size, full-travel keyboard.

To what extent can a portable computer encompass all of the above?

The Keyboard and Navigation

Fact: you can't miniaturize a high-performance computer to laptop dimensions without making certain compromises. Take the keyboard, for a start. The keyboard on a typical office PC is usually 18 inches wide. A laptop has to offer the same functionality in 12 inches. A sub-notebook has to do it in around $8\frac{1}{2}$ inches or less.

Actually, it *is* possible. What happens is that laptop keyboards double up certain key functions, or eliminate them entirely. The keyboard on most office computers, for example, has an alphanumeric pad on the far right. Laptop keyboards dispense with this, but allow you to access alphanumeric functions by pressing a separate function key that temporarily disables normal keyboard operation.

Then there's navigation. A normal **mouse**, for use with Windows-based software, isn't practical on a laptop. If you're traveling in, say, an aeroplane, there's usually not enough room to use the computer and a mouse together. Where would the mouse-mat go? You could end up accidentally massaging the knee of whoever was sitting next to you. So instead, various alternatives are used, some more successful than others.

A **tracker ball** is a sort of inverted mouse attached to the side of the computer, or placed just beneath the keyboard. Then there are **pen**-based systems that allow you to control functions, like pulling down menus or highlighting text, by touching an electronic pen to the screen. Then there's the **mouse button** – a pressure sensitive 'nipple' that sits in the middle of the keyboard. And, uniquely to Apple's top-end PowerBooks, is a pressure sensitive, solid state **TrackPad**.

None, in my opinion, is quite as good as a conventional mouse. (If they were, desktop PCs would have adopted them by now.) A very good way of testing them out, incidentally, is to try to play Solitaire, the electronic card game program which comes as standard with Windows. If you can't easily move the playing cards around with the pointing device, the odds are it will be just as difficult to shift blocks of text around and choose menus, too.

The Display

Desktop computers have **cathode ray tubes** (CRTs) as standard, almost exactly the same technology used by television sets. As might be expected, these are too heavy and power-hungry for laptops. Instead, LCD screens are used – a highly advanced version of the technology found in digital watches and calculators. What exactly are liquid crystals, and how do they work?

They were first discovered by an Austrian botanist in 1888 (there's one for your next Trivial Pursuit game). They're organic, originally from plants, and in their natural state, transparent, or vaguely opaque. There are three main types: smectic, nematic, and cholesteric. The ones in LCD screens are nematic, so called because their rod-like molecules are orientated parallel to one another (the Greek νεματοσ, *nematos*, means 'threadlike').

The primary characteristic of a nematic liquid crystal is that it's a procrastinator: it doesn't know whether it wants to be a solid or a liquid, and so spends its life in a sort of halfway house stage. For this reason, in the beginning botanists and physicists used to find studying them rather boring. It was rather like watching one of those people in TV commercials who endlessly debate with themselves over the merits of butter versus margarine without ever coming to a conclusion. So one day in 1960, a bored physicist decided to liven things up. He took some nematic liquid crystals and electrocuted them. The results had far reaching consequences.

Said scientist discovered that by passing an electric current through the crystals, the molecules all lined up into a helical structure which reflected any light whose wavelength was equivalent to the pitch of that helix. Then, when he switched off the current, they instantly lapsed back into their normal state and became transparent sluggards once more. After further study of several types of liquid crystal, he came up with a variety whose molecules lined up perpendicular to the oncoming light when charged. As a result, they blocked that light. Thus was born the concept of the LCD display.

A typical LCD screen has several hundred thousand little 'tanks' of liquid crystal, each connected to its own individual capacitor or transistor. A single capacitor/liquid crystal combination constitutes a pixel. There are three such pixels for color displays – red, green, and blue. Whenever the capacitor is turned on, its crystals become opaque. When several thousand of them are turned on and off at once and the combination is viewed from a distance, the illusion of solid images is created, as on a television screen.

The Display: Dual-Scan or TFT?

Until very recently, the majority of LCD screens were monochrome. The color varieties were just too expensive and bulky. But today, increasingly, color screens are becoming the norm. Doubtless within five years, black and white displays will be a distant memory, like black and white television sets. At the time of writing, there are essentially two varieties of LCD screen on offer: **dual-scan** and **TFT** (thin film transistor).

Dual-scan displays, as their name suggests, are made up of two LCD screens, placed one above the other. If you look closely, you can see the join. Because each screen is refreshed separately, the refresh rate of the combination is effectively doubled. In a nutshell, this means colors are brighter, and moving objects, such as the mouse cursor, are less likely to become blurred.

How does dual-scan compare to CRT? On monochrome screens, you won't notice any difference. On color screens, the results are usually not as sharp as those of typical desktop PCs. Not that you'll really be aware of this, unless you put the two together. But another, more significant, drawback of a dual-scan display is that the sandwich of LCD layers means the display can't easily be viewed from an angle. Therefore, if your job involves a lot of presentation work where several people have to be able to look at the screen at once, you might be better off with a TFT display – if you can afford it.

TFT is the most sophisticated LCD screen technology. And it's the most expensive, adding considerably to the cost of a laptop – at the moment, anyway. TFT screens also tend to be bulkier and consume more power than their counterparts. Where longevity and portability are factors, this might affect your choice of laptop. Another perceived disadvantage is that the image on many TFT color displays is degraded if too much light shines on its surface.

What are its advantages, then? Whereas other LCD screens are made up of matrices of interconnected capacitors, in TFT screens, the capacitors are replaced by transistors. Each pixel transistor is independent of the one directly next to it. The practical advantage of this is that there's no danger of so-called 'crosstalk' interference between pixels. This phenomenon can sometimes cause blurring and ghosting of fast moving objects on some of the cheaper screens. For instance, the cursor can sometimes disappear into the background, making (especially) Windows-based packages very irksome to use.

TFT overcomes this. Indeed, some TFT screens are getting to be as legible as CRTs. Some would say they surpass them.

Batteries

The bottom line is battery life. A laptop drained of power isn't a computer, it's just a useless box of chips.

There are three types of battery technology in general use. Some machines have **nickel cadmium** cells, the same sort of batteries found in the majority of camcorders, rechargeable shavers and mobile phones. As anyone who regularly uses these devices will probably be aware, you've got to take great care to completely discharge the battery before you recharge it. If you don't, the cell starts to hold less and less power as it's progressively recharged – the so-called memory effect.

A superior battery technology is **nickel metal hydride**, usually shortened to NiMH. Its great advantage over nickel cadmium is that it holds up to 80% more charge. On the downside, however, it takes somewhat longer to charge. And, like nickel cadmium, NiMH suffers from the memory effect and so has to be completely discharged before every recharge.

Which brings us to the new kid on the block, **nickel ion**. The average cell holds three times the charge of its nickel cadmium equivalent, and doesn't suffer from any memory effect. So you can effectively plug in and top up your laptop's charge whenever you happen to come across an AC outlet. For this reason, most manufacturers currently seem to be switching over to nickel ion technology.

At least, until something better comes along. Rumours abound of impending zinc–air technologies and even some variation on an astronaut's fuel-cell. These, it's said, will keep a laptop going all day and beyond. But I stress, these technologies haven't yet appeared on retailers' shelves.

So what's the best you can currently expect from a fully charged portable computer? At the time of writing, few laptops claim to live more than about five hours on a single battery. However, I find that even this figure can be something of an exaggeration. Yes, you can get five hours of battery life *if* you turn off the backlight, disable the hard disk, reduce the speed of the processor, and enable goodness knows how many other power management functions. But does anyone really want to work like this?

Probably a better, easier solution is just to buy a few spare batteries and always carry them on long trips. Some computers, the IBM Thinkpad range, for example, and the newer Apple PowerBooks, can now accommodate two batteries as a matter of course. The combination should last you the distance between London and New York, with a little power spare for any security checks at the other end. More on this theme anon.

When you talk to the computer salesperson, specify that your preferred laptop should be able to exchange batteries 'hot.' In other words, it must allow you to replace the batteries in mid-session without blowing a fuse or losing all the computer's data. Also, it's worth inquiring about buying an external battery charger. The majority of laptop manufacturers don't supply these themselves, and only allow you to recharge the batteries inside the computer itself, but a few third-party manufacturers do produce external rechargers for some of the more popular makes. Obviously, it's better if you can be using the laptop from one battery and be simultaneously recharging another battery (or batteries).

AC Power Supply

This is an important consideration. All portable computers will plug into the mains, of course. Problems can sometimes arise, however, if you travel abroad on a regular basis. This isn't just because plugs vary from country to country. Taking a travel adapter with you will easily solve these annoyances. No, the primary danger comes from the varieties of foreign AC supplies, some of which vary dramatically from what is the norm at home. The voltage in one country might be no problem at all; in another it might blow up your computer.

Basically, check that your laptop's **transformer** – the bit that converts AC into DC current – is able to cope with a range of voltages and currents. Turn it over and look on the back. If it says something along the lines of 'INPUT: 100–240V ~ 50/60 Hz,' then you're probably safe. This will cope with power supplies in the USA and all of Europe. If in doubt, *always* check with the manufacturer before plugging in to any exotic socket. Fried computer chips do not perform especially well.

Peripherals

A good laptop should offer the same sort of connectivity as the desktop PC. In other words, it must be able to link to devices like printers and modems. This means having so-called serial and parallel ports at the back. Also, because the most hassle-free way of transferring files between a laptop and a desktop computer is on floppy disk, you should ensure that your chosen portable has a floppy disk drive, either internal or external.

Another thing to look out for is the international standard, PCMCIA, mentioned earlier. The better, more flexible portable computers have at least one, usually two, PC Card slots. Into these, you can plug credit-card sized accessories like modems, network interfaces and memory.

A PC Card device is *theoretically* (note my italics) as interchangeable between computers as a VHS video cassette is between VCRs. In other words, a card taken from one computer can be plugged directly into another, and will function in exactly the same way. For this reason, these days, it really isn't worth buying a laptop that doesn't offer PC Card compatibility. Not that are many portable computers around that don't.

Notebook or Sub-notebook?

How big are your hands? In terms of functionality, today's note-books and sub-notebooks do much the same job. The only real difference is one of scale. A notebook tends to be about 12 inches wide, compared to $8\frac{1}{2}$ inches or $9\frac{1}{2}$ inches on a sub-notebook. So if you're a touch-typist with fingers the size of cucumbers, you'd probably be best advised to choose the for-mer machine.

The size of the display might also be a factor. At 6 inches or so, the screens on sub-notebooks tend to be OK for most appli-cations, like word processing or spreadsheets. However, if you want to run a program that's display-intensive, such as Desktop Publishing or a design package, you might find the screen *too* small. Likewise, if you're using the computer for pre-sentation work, where more than one person has got to be able to see it at the same time, you'll soon discover that 6 inches is not a hell of a lot of space.

Two Laptops

Because there are so many different types on the market, I can't possibly detail them all. In any case, as I said before, there's nothing to beat sitting down with a knowledgeable salesperson and having hands-on experience. Do *not* choose a laptop from a catalogue or magazine, basing your decision on price alone or recommendation from a friend. You yourself must be comfortable with the keyboard and all other aspects of the machine. You're not just investing money in your computer, you're entrusting your on-the-road business needs to it as well. If you are to perform to order, so must it.

That said, I'll look at just two portables, chosen quite simply because they *are* my favourites: the Compaq Concerto and the IBM Thinkpad. Between them they have, in my opinion, all the most desirable features of a perfect laptop.

The Compaq Concerto

At first glance, this battleship grey computer could easily be mistaken for one of those 1960s portable radios. It weighs in at 7 lbs and measures $12 \times 9 \times 2$ inches. The standard specification includes 4 Mbytes of RAM, a 120 Mbyte hard drive, a 25 MHz 486SL processor, a $9\frac{1}{2}$ inch display, and a nickel metal hydride battery giving 4 hours plus. There's also space for two PC Cards.

So far, it sounds like any other machine of its type, doesn't it? So what's the big deal?

Two things. First, the screen also doubles as an input and control device. You can operate all the menus, click on icons, and highlight text, simply by placing the integral pen on to the touch-sensitive screen and then tapping, lightly. As I said when I described the Sharp 9000, this is a much faster, more responsive way of accessing a computer's functions. Certainly more so than messing around with something like a tracker ball, especially if you're somewhere like an aircraft cabin, where elbow room is limited.

As an aside, the Concerto also comes bundled with handwriting recognition software. In other words you write directly on to the screen, the program analyses your handwriting, and like a pharmacist reading a doctor's prescription, best-guesses what you've actually written. This, however, I find of limited use. *I* often can't read my own handwriting, so it really would be too much to expect a machine to be able to cope. And, not surprisingly, it doesn't. Nevertheless, those with tidy, copperplate handwriting might be more successful.

The second major feature is that the inbuilt handle doubles as a screen stand and the slimline, detachable keyboard can be pulled out and fixed at an angle directly beneath. This allows the Concerto to be placed and used *comfortably* on an aircraft's fold-down table, even if you're traveling Economy. It's the only laptop that can be used in this way, making it ideal for long-haul, workaholic jetsetters.

IBM Thinkpad 755C

Probably the Rolls Royce of the portable computer world, with a price tag to match. From the outside, it doesn't look much at first. Measuring 11.7 × 8.3 × 2 inches and weighing 6.4 lbs, the Thinkpad's standard specification includes 4 Mbytes of RAM (expandable to 36), a 50 MHz 486DX processor, a 170 Mbyte hard disk (optional to 810 Mbytes), and a nickel metal hydride battery giving upwards of 4 hours. With power management facilities enabled, 8 hours of operation are claimed – and if you don't trust those claims, there's space for a second battery.

The Thinkpad has two outstanding features. The first has got to be its 10.4 inch color active matrix display, one of the largest and clearest on any laptop. I daresay there are some people who can tell the difference between this and a conventional CRT color screen, but I'm not one of them. Added to this is the computer's modular construction, allowing peripherals such as a TV tuner, CD-ROM drive, and so on, to be installed in seconds. They simply plug in; there's no messing around with cards or wires. The inbuilt microphone and quality speaker make the Thinkpad an excellent portable multimedia machine, too. Salespeople take note.

All in all, the Thinkpad is a laptop computer that out-performs most of those on the desk top. It's not cheap, however. Unless I were accompanied by presidential style security guards packing heavy-duty firearms, I think I might be somewhat wary about walking around in public with this machine.

Portable Printers

Must we discuss these? I'm not saying that **portable printers** are no good. Today, *some* produce letter quality output equal to that from desktop printers – albeit somewhat more lethargically. The point is, does it make any sense to travel with a portable printer? On what sorts of occasions do you *really* need to produce hard copy while away from the office?

Not in transit, that's for sure. On a plane or train, there's simply nowhere to put the damn printer. No, the only practical place to use a portable printer would be in your hotel bedroom. That said, in all the years I've been traveling with a laptop, all of my hotels, from three star up to five, have offered some sort of secretarial facilities where I could just hand in a floppy disk and get a printout five minutes later. And if I wasn't staying in a hotel, there's always been a business bureau nearby. In a later chapter I'll recount some problems I've faced on my travels which have led me to conclude that with perseverance you can get a printout anywhere in the world.

But my main argument against packing a portable printer is the bulk aspect. Not in itself, of course. Today, portable printers are no bigger than laptops, and getting smaller all the time. Nevertheless the combination of laptop, portable printer, paper, and power transformers – even if you can shoehorn them all into a single briefcase – is enough to make you develop a physique like someone out of *Muscle & Fitness Magazine*. Then you might be tempted to start kicking sand in people's faces instead of concentrating on the job.

On the other hand, maybe you've *got* to produce a presentation by next morning. Or perhaps you're the type who likes to be independent of the hotel or business bureau setup; who prefers the idea of being self-contained and ready for any eventuality, like Batman with his all-purpose utility belt.

Very well. What, then, should you look for in a portable printer?

It should have the same characteristics as the ideal laptop: compactness, light weight, the same sort of immunity to baggage handlers, and a battery with sufficient staying-power to produce a day's worth of documentation. Added to that, its printed output ought to be such that no-one confuses it with a fax or a dot matrix printer, and the paper should emerge at a rate that doesn't require its owner to take an extended coffee break between paragraphs. In other words, the portable should perform exactly as a desktop printer, and produce the same sort of quality.

Do any oblige? Here, I have to be ultra-critical. Thus far, I *personally* have only come across two machines that I would ever trust to travel with me and produce decent copy. By 'decent,' I mean printed copy that wouldn't damage my reputation as a businessman. That isn't to say that other machines, just as good, don't exist, however. As always in these cases, don't take my word for it; check with your friendly computer dealer.

Canon BJ-10sx

Canon's **BJ-10sx** offers a print speed of up to 110 characters per second (cps) and an intuitive user control panel. Its size and appearance aren't too overwhelming. The BJ-10sx measures $12.2 \times 8.7 \times 1.9$ inches, which means it just about fits into a briefcase along with a laptop, so long as it's used with the optional 9.5 volt ni-cad battery pack rather than the AC adapter. And at just 3.7 lbs, it's quite a lightweight.

The whole thing is nicely constructed with no protruding edges. The clamshell lid on top opens up to function as a single-sheet paper tray for letter and legal size paper, while a second, detachable paper cover immediately below this opens out to reveal the print-head. Turn the machine upside down and you'll find a secondary feed mechanism for envelopes, transparencies, or thick substrates such as label sheets. To use this it's necessary to open out the printer stand, recessed into the back, which also conceals the battery compartment.

Setting up and getting started are a breeze. Once the 64-nozzle ink cartridge has been clipped on and primed, the paper drops into the back, is aligned against the size guides, and is moved into the correct position with the paper-advance button. The control panel itself is well laid out with six buttons and three LEDs, and shouldn't cause anyone any problems. The buttons stand just proud of the surface of the printer and have a nice, positive feel to them. If errors do occur, these are indicated by a series of beeps and flashes.

And performance? The BJ-10sx runs smoothly and quietly. In letter quality mode at 360×360 dpi, the characters are well-defined, neither too dense nor too light. Indeed, I think it would be difficult for anyone but an expert to tell the difference between this and laser output. The printer has three emulations. In other words you can flick a button and make it think it's a popular desktop printer. The emulations include IBM Proprinter X24E, Canon BJ-130e, and Epson LQ-510,

Verdict: well designed and a good overall performer. A machine that exudes quality.

DeskJet Portable

Everyone expected Hewlett Packard's DeskJet Portable to be simply a mini-version of their well-established desktop machine. However the big surprise is its appearance – smoothly rectangular and finished in a dark, gunmetal grey. Up-end the thing and it looks like that obelisk at the beginning of the film *2001*. Futuristic is the word. In normal use the printer sits upright, supported by a swivel stand recessed into the back. In this position, its controls are up at the top. There are six buttons and six small LEDs. As well as controlling the normal printing functions, these are also used to set the configuration.

The DeskJet Portable measures $12 \times 2.5 \times 5.75$ inches and weighs in at around 4.4 lbs. It easily passes the briefcase test, even leaving room for the rather bulky AC adapter. But if you don't want to take that on the road with you, the 6 volt ni-cad battery is supposed to be good for about 100 A4 pages, which should cope with a corporate report and a few letters to the board. Top print speeds are 167 cps for letter quality and 240 cps for draft, except in battery mode when draft drops to 167 cps in order to conserve power.

Hewlett Packard have designed a remarkably effective paper feed mechanism. Stick a sheet of paper in the back slit and it's automatically grabbed by rollers, fed through, and positioned with complete precision under the print head ready for the off. The output looked exactly the same as that from a standard DeskJet printer. Which isn't surprising, as it uses the same ink cartridge and delivers the same resolution – 300 dpi (300 × 150 dpi in draft mode).

The DeskJet Portable comes with four inbuilt fonts – CG Times, Letter Gothic, Univers, and Courier. There's also an optional, slightly difficult to attach, sheet feeder which complements the machine so completely that the combination could easily be taken for a separate desktop machine in its own right. Indeed, some people use it in exactly this way.

Before I leave the subject of printers, there's one handy tip I should pass on. If you're traveling without a printer but need hard copy, why not simply send a fax from your laptop to the hotel's fax machine, and then pick up the printed pages from reception? OK, it won't be 'letter quality,' but it's perfectly adequate if you just want to produce notes that are going to be referred to in a meeting.

Modems

If you want to use your portable computer to keep in touch with home or the office, then a modem is *the* one essential peripheral.

The word is derived from its function: MODulator/ DEModulator. It turns computer data (your word-processed document, for example), which is digital, into a series of squawks and hisses (analog data) that can be transmitted, in the same way as your voice, over a conventional telephone line. Once these modulated squawks and hisses reach the other end, another modem turns them back into digital data (demodulates them, in other words) and feeds the information into the attached computer.

Most likely, you've been using a modem for years without realizing it. It's in fact the central component of a fax machine – the bit that whistles when you first phone up. Indeed, essentially you can look upon a modem as nothing more than a naked fax machine; one stripped of its scanner and printer. Unfortunately, while facsimile has acquired the reputation of being simple, push-button technology, to many, modem communications have assumed the status of a Black Art.

Actually, modems *per se* have never really been the problem. A modem is just a dumb box of chips that responds to whatever the computer software tells it to do. Then it sends the signal, via an attached wire, into the telephone system. It's this software, or more properly, the way in which it communicated with the modem, that used to cause all the grief.

Until very recently, the interface and operation were unnecessarily complicated, the province of so-called 'comms gurus.' These people used to talk about modems and communications software 'handshaking' and 'negotiating a protocol.' So much so that they often made it sound as if a member of the UN Security Council was stuck somewhere on your hard drive.

Today, however, modern software – be it fax software, a terminal program, or a dedicated comms package, like **WinCIM** for CompuServe – makes communicating with the modem a relatively simple, menu-driven operation. In the initial stages, anyway. When you first install your program, it usually prompts you with a list of modems, and asks you to select which is yours, or most closely resembles yours. Having done that, all you then have to do is select the speed at which you wish to communicate, and the telephone number you want to dial. Consequently, communicating by modem has become virtually as straightforward as sending a fax.

Except, of course, when it comes to traveling abroad. But before we get to that, the first question is: what should you look for when choosing a modem? As before, I can only give basic pointers. Your eventual choice should be between you and your salesperson.

Fax Modem or Standard?

No contest. My advice would be always to go for a modem with fax capability, even if you think you won't need it. These days, anyway, those that don't offer this feature are becoming increasingly rare. Used in combination with good fax software, such as Delrina's **WinFax** (many fax modems come bundled with such a fax software package as a matter of course), a fax modem allows you to create a document on your word processor and then fax it directly to someone else's fax machine without having to print it out first. Likewise, when someone faxes a document to you, your fax modem receives it and automatically displays it on your computer screen. Again, without you having to print it out.

One point to note, incidentally. You can't edit a document that comes through a fax modem into your laptop, any more than you can edit a paper-based fax. A facsimile image received in this manner is exactly that: an image; a graphical representation of the original document. You can, however, feed it through optical character recognition (**OCR**) software and convert it into editable text. This I shall touch on at a later stage.

Pocket or PC Card?

There are two types of modem used by laptop-equipped travelers: **pocket modems**, which are external devices, and PC Card modems, that plug directly into the computer. Which is for you?

A pocket modem, as its name suggests, is usually about the size of a pocket calculator. Most are powered by a couple of AA batteries, with AC power as an option. You attach it to your computer by a serial lead, which plugs into the laptop's serial port, at the back. The modem usually has some sort of

LCD or LED display on the front, to let you know such things as the speed of connection, whether or not it's dialing out, when a connection has been made, if someone is phoning you up, and so on. Most have inbuilt loudspeakers, too, allowing you to hear the dialing and comms operations as they're carried out.

Indeed, it's this audio-visual indication of what's going on that's usually cited as one of the main reasons for buying a pocket modem. That, and the fact that a pocket modem is easily interchangeable between your desktop PC and your laptop. One device will service both, so you don't have to buy two modems. On the other hand, it's one extra item of equipment that you have to carry with you in addition to your laptop and all its peripherals; one that could possibly get mislaid. Do you need the hassle?

No? OK, let's look at the credit-card size PCMCIA of modems – or PC Card devices – which plug directly into PC Card slots in the computer. They take their power from the laptop itself, which means there are no batteries or electrical outlets to bother with. Thus a laptop and PC Card modem combination is extremely compact and lightweight. You just plug an external telephone line into a socket on the side of the little modem, and the two of you are ready for action.

But beware. Configuring a PC Card modem – or any PC Card peripheral, for that matter – with your computer system can *sometimes* be as long-winded a procedure as filling out a mortgage application. You need to install so-called Card and Socket Devices software and then coax everything into life. Sometimes, it isn't exactly a non-trivial procedure. Even the PCMCIA's founder once admitted taking over five hours to get his fax modem to work with his laptop. Normally, though, it can be done in a few minutes, and thereafter will work as well, if not better, than an external modem.

Incidentally, the forthcoming IBM OS/2 Warp operating system and Microsoft's Windows 95 will configure PCMCIA devices automatically, so soon there'll be none of this hassle.

Hayes Compatibility

Named after the inventor of the first direct connection modem, Dennis C. Hayes. These days, it's unlikely you'll ever find a modem that *isn't* Hayes compatible to some degree. Therefore, unless you're the type who buys his computer peripherals from obscure little antique shops, this isn't going to be a problem.

The Hayes standard refers to the basic codes, now accepted by manufacturers worldwide, used by the computer's communications software to control the modem. 'AT,' for example, says to the modem 'Attention' or 'Wake up!', and announces that more commands are on their way. 'ATDT 999' says 'Attention: dial 999, using **tone dialing**.' I'll go into more detail in a later chapter.

Don't worry about these codes, by the way. For the most part, modern software shields you from them, in much the same way that Windows shields you from the bad old MS-DOS Command Line Interface. It's only when you have to tinker with them slightly, as we'll see, that they become an issue.

Speed

Not mph but **bps** – 'bits per second'. These 'bits' are pieces of computer information, corresponding to characters and control codes. The more of them that can be shifted down the telephone line in any one second, the faster the modem, and the less time (and money) you'll spend on the phone. Speed is especially a factor if you have to make a lot of expensive point to point international calls.

One thing to bear in mind: just as the top speed of a marine convoy is that of its slowest frigate, the top speed of a modem connection is that of the slowest modem in that connection. So if you've got a 14 400 bps modem but your contact only has a 2400 bps model, the top speed at which you can send data to them, and they to you, will be 2400 bps.

So what speed modem should you be looking for? My advice is, don't waste your money on anything slower than 14 400 bps. That's usually called V32bis, and is the top rate currently supported by most of the major CompuServe nodes internationally.

V32 *what*? I'm sorry. This issue is clouded more than a little by modem-speak. Manufacturers talk about V21 modems, V32 modems, V42bis, and even V34 (once called V.FAST) modems. For the record, V21 means 300 bps, V32 means 9600 bps, V32bis means 14 400 bps, while V34 is an astounding 28 800 bps. Faster throughput rates are achieved by using different types of **data compression**. Note, however, that these high speeds are dependent on having a clear, interference-free telephone line. If there's noise on the line – and there usually is, to some degree – the modem will automatically drop down to a slower speed.

So, to backtrack, which one is for you? The general advice – and mine – is, go for the fastest modem you can afford, even though the online service to which you're trying to connect might not necessarily support such a high rate of knots. Don't worry; in time, it probably will. But in any case, nowadays, buying a high-speed modem will not burn a hole in anyone's pocket. Even a V32bis modem costs as little as a decent dinner for two plus wine. Starve a little.

Compression and Error Correction

These days, the two go hand in hand. I alluded to compression above. The way to squeeze higher speeds out of a modem is to ally it to some sort of data compression/**error correction** algorithm. Two to look out for are **MNP5** and **V42 bis**.

A modem incorporating MNP5 can yield compression ratios of up to 2:1, depending on the sort of data being transmitted. So long as you're connected to another, similarly equipped modem. In other words, if you connect a V32 (9600 bps) modem that has inbuilt MNP5 compression to another, identical device, you should be able to coax speeds of up to 19 200 bps between the two. V42bis can achieve compression ratios of up to 4:1. So, a V32 modem with inbuilt V42bis compression will, on a good day, yield 38 400 bps.

The V42 standard also incorporates error correction facilities. Error correction is essential on a modem in order to overcome breaks in transmission and data flow caused by such factors as line noise or cross-line interference. To put it very simply, what happens is that data is transmitted in a series of blocks, each series a set length. The send modem says to the receive modem something along the lines of, 'I've just sent you 32 blocks of data. Did you get them all?' If it did, the receive modem sends back a message saying, 'All received OK. Please send the next block.'

However, if, in mid-transmission, a bird lands on the line, the operator butts in, or something else disrupts the flow, then the receive modem will say, 'Sorry. Didn't quite catch that. Can you send them again please?' Thereupon the send modem re-transmits until the blocks are transmitted successfully. Error correction standards in general use include MNP 2, 3 and 4, V42, and Link Access Procedure for Modems (LAP/M).

Yes, I know they sound like complete gobbledegook. But so, on the face of it, do the nutrients in a breakfast cereal. Just as you know your cornflakes ought to contain niacin, thiamine, and vitamin B, so your modem ought to have beneficial ingredients like MNP4 and V42.

Some modems – even by the same manufacturer – are better than others at coping with noisy telephone lines. Some are happier sending and receiving facsimile images than others. As with computers and palmtops, if you're unsure (and I can't stress this enough) the best way to choose is to get a knowledgeable computer dealer to go through things with you. A good one will show you how to configure a PC Card modem for your particular system and will be prepared to risk the price of a phone call and dial your own particular online service, office modem, or fax machine just to make sure you're happy with the results. It's your money – insist.

* * *

OK, let's assume you've bought all your equipment and it works to spec. Now you're off on your travels. But pause awhile. Just as you make a checklist before you jet off on holiday (Aspirins? Suntan lotion? Have you canceled the newspapers?), so you should take a few minutes to think about potential problems that might arise when traveling with your laptop. Which takes me on to the next chapter.

2: Planes, Trains, and Automobiles – and Boats

Checklist and Essentials

It's often a good idea to make a check list of all of your computer's essential peripherals before you set off to make sure they're packed. Obviously, landing in New York and then finding you've left, say, the external floppy drive or power transformer in London can cause considerable frustration. But this is just common sense. Apart from making such a list, what other precautions might it be advisable to take before setting off?

1. If your laptop is a new machine, make sure you play around with it extensively before taking it abroad. Get used to how it works and its various foibles. Especially, check that peripherals such as the floppy disk drive and the modem are working to spec. You don't want to come across any sudden problems or surprises while stranded in somewhere remote, like Timbuktu. However, if your computer is one of the big-name brands, the chances are that – within reason – anywhere you go in the world, there'll be a local support centre that you can telephone for help, sometimes with a toll-free number. Make a note of all such telephone numbers before you set off and keep them separate from the computer.

2. How are you going to carry the computer and its peripherals? In the padded shoulder bag that came with the computer, perchance? Very well. But will it fit everything, disks and adapters included? In my experience, not all

dedicated computer bags do. But if it does, as a test, load everything up before you go, including power transformers and adapters (it's surprising how heavy these can be), and walk round the block a few times. If you get shoulder ache after just a hundred yards, imagine what it's going to be like on the road, sauntering between airport terminals and running after cabs.

So is it possible to ditch anything? If not, you might at least be able to do something about that brick-sized power transformer. Some companies now supply smaller, lighter replacement versions for the more popular makes of laptop. Consider investing in one if your physique isn't quite up to Arnold Schwarzenegger proportions.

One thing to bear in mind about computer bags, incidentally, especially if you're traveling by air. These days, airlines are getting very strict about the number of bags you can take onboard. Some say just one piece of hand-luggage, not exceeding $20 \times 10 \times 5$ inches. Others say two bags. Whatever, if you're already carrying a suit-bag and a briefcase, your laptop's shoulder bag will put you over the limit (and possibly in traction, too). The best solution, therefore, it to go to a luggage shop and buy one of those floppy shoulder bags that will accommodate your computer, its peripherals, and whatever would normally go into your briefcase.

If you're the owner of a Mac PowerBook, you might consider a case called a 'WetSuit.' A satisfied customer enthuses: 'The WetSuit has been the most useful addition to my PowerBook over the last few years. It's basically made of the same rubberized material as aquatic wetsuits, and fits snugly round the machine, even when open. It gives a nice bit of padding to the PowerBook, without adding much bulk. I've carried the machine in its WetSuit in my soft fabric shoulder bag for the last couple of years, with no problem. The computer has been adequately protected without the need for special computer luggage.'

3. Always take a supply of blank floppy disks, pre-formatted if possible. But can't you buy them overseas? you ask. Of course you can, but try checking into a hotel – any hotel – at, say, 10.00 pm in the evening and then realizing you're disk-less. What do you do? Apart from anything else, if you've been working in transit, it helps if you can save your files to floppy disk periodically, just in case anything untoward happens to you or laptop before you arrive.

4. Always take a **boot disk** with you, carrying all the system files required to boot the computer from the floppy drive. It doesn't happen very often, but your hard disk's boot sector – the programs that tell the computer what it is, how to start up, its operating system, etc – can sometimes get corrupted. Even though all the other files on the hard disk might be perfectly OK, the fact of not being able to boot up means you can't access them. With a boot disk, however, you can at least copy them off the hard drive and take them across to a replacement computer.

    If you're using an IBM-compatible laptop, to create a boot disk from the C:> prompt in MS-DOS, put a floppy disk into the internal drive (usually drive a:) and type:

    C:>format a: /s

    This both formats the floppy and copies the systems files across. There are programs, such as Norton Utilities, which make this much more of a push-button operation. I'd therefore advise you go for one of those if possible.

5. By the same token, always carry backup copies of your most important files on floppy disk. Don't pack them in

the same case as your laptop, though, just in case it gets impounded or stolen. Some would say that it's a good idea to bring backup copies of your application files, such as word processor and spreadsheet, too, in case anything goes wrong with the copies on your hard disk. I'd disagree here, if only because, these days, the average Windows-based application takes up at least 10 disks. So if you've got a spreadsheet, database, word processor, and presentations program, for instance, you'll need an extra suitcase just to carry the original disks.

6. Remember to pack your international power adapter. If it's got extras that allow you to plug into lightbulb and shaver sockets, so much the better.

7. It's a good idea to take an AC extension cord with you. Even in some five star hotels, you can often be surprised at how far the writing desk is from the nearest available power socket. An extension cord means you can work, or recharge, anywhere in the room.

8. It's also a good idea to pack a power surge protector, available from outlets such as Tandy in the UK or Radio Shack in the USA, particularly if you're traveling somewhere whose electricity supply is dubious. This fits between the laptop's plug and the AC socket and guards against electricity spikes, some of which can be strong enough to fry the innards of a computer. Also, it helps protect against power-line surges caused by lightning striking the electricity cables, apparently quite common in tropical climes. It's always better to be safe than sorry.

9. Pack a screwdriver. I personally don't recommend on-the-road surgery if something goes seriously wrong with your laptop. Sometimes, however, the problem can be as simple as a wire coming loose. In which case, you should be able to cope on your own.

10. Tape your business card or address to the side of the laptop. Then, if it's mislaid, an honest citizen might find it, read your address details, and return it to you. Unlikely, I agree, but it's always best to look on the optimistic side.

11. Carry a copy of this book with you. Even if you don't use it for reference, you can at least jam it under the leg of a wobbly table and effect a temporary cure. And if you ever do find yourself bookless, I'm sure it beats reading the care labels on your clothes.

* * *

Insurance and Maintenance

Alluded to above. Whenever the subject of traveling with a laptop comes up, I'm always put in mind of that British RAF officer who, in the middle of the Gulf War, left his portable computer on the back seat of his car while he went somewhere. He was only gone about five minutes, but when he returned, he found that the thing had been stolen. What made matters far worse, however, was that its hard disk included a copy of preliminary Allied invasion plans of Kuwait. Fortunately, everything turned out OK. The thief was highly patriotic, and returned the computer, and its data, intact. Eventually.

Unfortunately, not all thieves are so public-spirited. Indeed, because they're so lightweight, and easy to steal and to 'fence', laptops are regarded by the insurance industry as something of a bad risk, like expensive jewelry and teenage motorcyclists. Some companies refuse to insure them at all, or insist they be included in a policy with all your other office equipment.

Even if they are, though, beware. You might be required to apply for a 'temporary removal extension' before you're covered for taking your computer on the road, especially if it's out of the country. The insurance company might even impose a hefty extra premium, sometimes as much as 5% of the computer's value, depending on where you're going and for how long. Virtually all of them will have an exclusion clause, stating that if the computer is left unattended in a car and gets stolen, then tough – no payout.

So check the small print in the insurance policy document very, very carefully. A number of policies will claim to cover all electrical equipment, including camcorders, tape recorders, and so on. Many people therefore assume that this blanket coverage will also extend to their portable computers. Not necessarily. In particular, see if there's a 'business use' get-out clause. If there is, this means that anything that could conceivably be used for business purposes, like electronic calculators, mobile phones, and laptops, is not included in the policy. After all, they'd argue, what possible reason could you have for traveling with a laptop if not for your job? Playing Solitaire, maybe?

Given the possible insurance pitfalls, is there anything you can do to your computer to make it less attractive to a thief – apart from disguising it as one of those early Apple 'portables' that weighed a ton?

1.   You could security mark it with an indelible pen whose special ink can only be read under fluorescent light, and put a large sticker on the front declaring that you've taken this measure. Most laptop thefts are usually carried out by opportunistic morons, though, so they probably wouldn't notice this until they'd actually made off with the machine.

2.   Some laptops – I'm thinking in particular of the larger Toshibas – have fold-down security rings on the side that allow them to be bolted to furniture and fittings. Like bicycle locks, however, they're no deterrent to the really determined thief.

3.   Install a burglar alarm. I know of two types: one plugs directly into the serial or printer port; the other fits into

the disk drive. They contain small, battery-operated motion detectors that screech like a tom cat unless disabled first of all with a special key. They're similar in principle to those security cassettes that fit into VCRs, and can usually be obtained from the larger computer peripheral mail order stores.

4.   Store the machine not in its brand-name padded shoulder bag but in a nondescript supermarket carrier bag.

Data Security

But let's suppose you're resigned to the fact that at some point the computer could get stolen. Maybe just as important to you as the hardware is the security of its data. Maybe, like the aforementioned RAF officer, you too are holding important military information on your hard disk. How do you safeguard the information?

1.   Virtually all the high-end business packages, like word processors, spreadsheets, and databases, now include password protection, either for individual files or the programs themselves. When you invoke such a password, the data in the file becomes encrypted, such that none but a really specialized computer hacker can get at it. Do ensure that you make a note of the password, and keep it separate from the computer.

2.   Choose a laptop with a removable hard disk. If you're leaving the computer anywhere, such as the boot of a car or an office drawer, you can take the disk out and carry it in your pocket.

3.   Consider buying a laptop that has a built-in **BIOS** password protection. Here, unless you enter the correct password, the computer won't even boot up. On some of the

more sophisticated models, you can security protect specific drives or directories.

4. Buy a hardware key or '**dongle**,' that fits into the laptop's serial or printer port. These are available from a number of computer peripheral stores. Unless the key is plugged in, the computer simply won't work. A bit of a nuisance if you lose the dongle, though.

On-site Maintenance

Although the majority of laptops are guaranteed for at least a year, should they fail, you're usually required to ship them back, not to the manufacturer, but to the dealer for repair. Exceptions include AST, Compaq, IBM, and Toshiba. Here, you can ship the computer to the company's local office, not just nationally, but anywhere in the world. Unfortunately, there's often no guarantee when the machine will be returned to you.

For an extra charge, however, some manufacturers, and most dealers, are prepared to offer some sort of on-site maintenance contract, where the laptop is either fixed there and then, or else replaced with one that works. Most such contracts are only valid within the country of purchase. But increasingly, manufacturers are waking up to the fact that, because laptop-equipped travelers tend to travel internationally, some sort of international scheme is required, too. A few have already taken the hint.

AST, for one, offers a service called Execare, which covers your laptop anywhere in mainland Europe, the USA, and most of the Far East. On phoning the local AST office, you can either get a replacement machine sent by courier and your dead one collected within 24 hours, or send your own machine to them by courier, and have it returned, good as new, usually within a couple of days.

As I said, most manufacturers are now beginning to realize the need to offer some sort of universal cover so, if you travel abroad a lot, the best thing to do is contact the individual dealer at the time of purchase and see what's on offer.

* * *

The above are the obvious precautions you can take before you start traveling. Other potential problems can be less easy to pre-empt. The vagaries of Customs and Excise, Security, Immigration, and so on, can often be dictated by the whims of specific bureaucrats and officials. This being so, in the next section I've included a few on-the-road examples by fellow travelers.

Customs and Excise Clearance

So, you have your shiny new laptop and you plan to travel abroad with it. The question is, will you be able to get the thing back into the country again on your return? This question is especially pertinent if you're entering Europe from the United States. For reasons that have never been adequately explained to me, in the US, computers only cost about half the price they do in, say, the UK. Many Europeans therefore try to take advantage of this by combining their American holiday with a spot of PC purchasing. Ever alert to this, customs officials lie in wait in the Green Channel, waiting to pounce on anything smelling of silicon.

So what's the best way of proving that the computer you're bringing into the country is the same one you took out? Some would say always travel with the receipts. Others maintain that taking out an official customs document – a **carnet** – and having it stamped at each port of entry and exit is the more sensible approach. This is less likely to be thought of as a forgery, as it can be verified fairly easily with a few international telephone calls. Unfortunately, carnets often cause more problems than they solve. I'm indebted to Mr Alan Dunsmuir for the following cautionary tale.

'I recently had to take a trip from London to San Francisco, then on to Montreal, before finally returning to London. My employer (or rather his data processing legal expert and his shipping agent working in tandem) insisted I get a carnet and have it processed at each airport.

'At London Heathrow the official was cynically amused, but I got my stamp, wasting only twenty minutes in the process. At San Francisco, the Customs Official in the Arrivals Hall looked at me quizzically and stamped the carnet with his normal "Cleared" stamp, refusing to read it or consider that anything else was needed. After a 10-hour flight and still needing to pick up a rented car and drive to my Hotel in a city I had never before visited, I was in no mood to argue with him.

'It was on the leg to Montreal that it really all fell apart. I had an early morning (around 06.00 am) flight to Toronto, with a connection there for Montreal. Early morning San Francisco to Toronto was clearly considered by the airport staff to be an internal flight, since other than asking to see my passport at the check-in desk there were no customs formalities to pass through. I showed the girl my carnet and asked if I could have it stamped.

'Her lip curled. "Look – It's 5.30am," she said. "You want me to leave my desk here and all these passengers waiting to check in, and take a car ride with you to another building at the far end of the airport, and wake up the customs staff when we get there, *just* so that you get your form stamped? Look at the people behind you. Half of them are carrying laptops! Do you think they all have forms to be stamped?"

'I got the distinct impression that the expected answer to the questions she had asked me was not "Yes." So I just passed through, unstamped.

'At the other end, I showed my carnet to Customs when leaving Montreal for London. But they said that since it carried no record of the laptop ever having arrived in Canada ("No, sir – San Francisco doesn't count as Canada . . . yet") they couldn't certify it as being re-exported. I didn't even try anything on arrival at Heathrow, but simply walked through the Green Channel as always.

'We then sent off the carnet for processing, and its semi-filled status kept our agent in full employment for about six weeks, and caused him so much trouble, that a new Company edict was issued shortly thereafter. "If you are planning an overseas trip with a laptop, we shall be pleased to issue a letter confirming ownership of the laptop and certifying that its original place of sale and normal place of use is the UK. **On no account attempt to raise and process a carnet for the laptop.**"'

So there you have it. Carry a letter from your employer, plus a copy of the original receipt. Those should serve you well enough throughout most of the western world, and other parts besides.

Security

It goes without saying, of course, that you should never pack anything delicate, like a portable computer, in your suitcase. It should always travel in your hand luggage. Which is where the inevitable problems can come in. Mike Maughan tells the following story.

'In February 1989, two months after the Lockerbie bombing, I took a Compaq portable on a round-the-houses trip to Canada and the US. My itinerary was Manchester, England to Toronto, Canada via Air Canada; Toronto to Atlanta,

Georgia via Eastern Airlines; Atlanta to Washington DC via American Airlines and finally Philadelphia to Manchester via British Airways.

'Security at Manchester wasn't bothered – they were happy to X-ray the machine. Toronto going to the US were more worried about whether I was going somewhere to work with it (I wasn't); Eastern Airlines didn't like me working on the machine in flight (anyway they went bust a week later!). Atlanta to DC didn't even X-ray the bags!

'When we came to check in at Philadelphia for our return flight to UK, however, the fun started. I had to open up the Compaq, demonstrate it was working and allow them (after X-ray) to see the battery pack removed. We then waited as our outbound flight was delayed for $4\frac{1}{2}$ hours.

'During this time I was called back to security no less than five times for more questions, including a requirement that I ran one of their programs on it (I declined as their disk was not virus-checked), more X-rays, a demand I surrender the machine to them for "investigation" (I refused, but offered to accompany it with them if necessary) and an attempt to dismantle the unit on the counter-top (which I again stopped). Their final bid was to tell me to check it in as hold luggage (oh yeah!), but of course they wouldn't be responsible for insurance, etc. I finally was allowed to take it on-board, where no-one took any notice of it whatsoever!'

Not an isolated tale by any means. Anyone who regularly takes to the air in the company of a portable computer and its peripherals should get used to being treated as a potential terrorist. Seen through the haze of an airport's X-ray equipment, the tightly packed combination of a laptop, modem, batteries, assorted wires, telephone plugs, and mouse positively exudes explosive possibilities.

My own experience is that nine out of ten times, I get stopped and the officials will request a physical examination of my computer. Not only will they want to look at it, and possibly inside it, they will usually insist that I switch the thing on and allow it to boot up. So I always – always – make life easy for them. I ensure that my battery is fully charged before I pass through Security. If it's dead, and the laptop remains lifeless, Security could summon personnel with flak-jackets to violate its data integrity. At the very least, they'll take it away and have somebody of dubious technical expertise poke at it.

But maybe I get hassled simply because I look suspicious. Others seem to have no problems whatsoever. 'My own experience,' says one fortunate soul, 'carrying a laptop in a shoulder bag through over 200 trips, is that I've only been asked to remove the machine and power it up on two occasions: in Houston and Dallas, Texas. Maybe I've just been lucky, but I haven't seen them make any other folks demo their portables, either.'

X-rays

On the subject of X-ray examination, incidentally, I'd like to dispose of one common urban myth. You sometimes hear tales of people putting their laptops through the airport X-ray machines. When they get it back at the other end, so the stories go, all its data has been erased or the computer has been rendered non-functional, its chips fried by the radiation.

Bunkum.

X-rays *cannot* erase magnetic data. Nor do they pose any danger to modern electronics. There are some types of circuits (mostly used in prototyping) that can be erased by X-rays, but none of these make it into the finished product. Anyway, laptop manufacturers routinely test their designs for sensitivity to such hazards as may be encountered in normal travel, and have published the results. They don't want any high-profile business executives suing them because a vital company report has suddenly been erased from the hard disk.

There is, however, one hazard related to airport X-ray machines, but it's not the X-rays themselves that are the problem. On some of the older models, the ones usually found in third world or former 'Eastern Bloc' countries, the motor's roller mechanism may be inadequately shielded, and generate enough residual magnetism to *possibly* cause damage. If you're worrying about this, there are two courses of action. First, insist the computer be examined by hand. If they don't agree, place it in the dead centre of the belt as it goes through the machine. Here, it's unlikely to come in close proximity to the motors.

Metal Detectors

Now these *can* cause damage, because you're walking through what is in effect the equivalent of a giant AC-powered electro-magnet. As an experiment, try running a conventional magnet along the surface of one of your floppy disks, and see what happens. Better still, don't. The thing is, you shouldn't really be going through a metal detector while carrying anything metallic like a laptop or palmtop, anyway. It will only cause the alarm to go beep, requiring a physical examination. Then again, maybe the idea of being frisked by a burly security officer turns you on, so go for it. But if you get your data erased, you've only got yourself to blame.

Terror at 20 000 Feet

So, you've survived the security checks, have made it to the plane, and now you want to use the computer while airborne. Are you sure?

Before you set off, while in the office, try this little experiment. Draw up your chair so it's two inches from the desk. Pull your computer's keyboard so far forward that you have to bend your wrists through 45 degrees to type. Comfortable? Finally, position a loudish, heavy-duty vacuum cleaner immediately beneath your chair so that its motor vibrations are transmitted up through your backside. That's the equivalent of traveling Club Class while using a laptop.

To simulate Economy, bring your chair two inches *further* forward, jam your knees underneath the desk, tuck your elbows into your sides, and balance the keyboard so it's hanging halfway over the edge of your desk and wobbles with each keystroke. For extra verisimilitude, bring a dozen screaming two year olds into the office and have them spill orange juice over you at half hourly intervals.

Now try programming a spreadsheet or writing a company report.

I'm not saying it's impossible to work in a plane, I'm simply saying it can be bloody difficult. If traveling Economy, try to get an aisle seat when you check in. Here, at least you'll have more elbow room than if you're squeezed in the middle or right up against the window. Then try to avoid the obvious onboard distractions, such as the complimentary drinks, the inflight movie, or the person in the next seat who wants to show you their holiday snaps.

If you can cope with this sort of thing – and many can't – the next question is: will the cabin staff allow you to start up your computer?

Many airlines now seem to be taking an increasingly belligerent stance against laptops. None has actually accused computer users of knocking planes out of the sky, but the implication is there, nonetheless. SAS, for example, has banned their use inflight, while United Airlines and American Airlines, amongst others, say you can't boot up for 15 minutes either side of takeoff and landing.

The main problem is radio wave emission. Everything electronic produces radio waves, of course. With a bit of application, for instance, you can readily turn a food processor into a rudimentary transmitter and broadcast soufflés from your kitchen. However, culinary emissions are a danger to no-one. You're unlikely ever to scramble the navigational equipment of another kitchen coming at you at 500 mph from a westerly direction. But in an aeroplane, it could be a totally different matter.

'While flying my plane, I turned on my laptop to test a navigational program,' reports the pilot of a light-aircraft. 'Suddenly, there was a 35 degree swing in the VOR (Visual Omni Range), and the aircraft, on autopilot, swung and banked right into restricted airspace.'

Larger planes might be just as susceptible. Recently, the US newspapers reported the case of a United Airlines 757 attempting a night landing. Everything was fine, until one of the laptop-equipped passengers in a second row seat tried saving his file to hard disk.

According to a crew member, 'The VOR and ILS (Instrument Landing System) needles started swinging like crazy. The Captain had to quickly go into manual. We were lucky that no serious damage was done.'

How can this be, given all the international regulations governing electronic equipment and potential interference? In the USA, for example, all laptops, by law, have to pass what are called FCC-A guidelines, which put an upper limit on their permitted radio wave emissions. Actually, most easily pass the much more stringent FCC-B guidelines. The fact is, portable computers *per se* don't seem to be the problem. Apparently it's their peripherals that could send you into a tail-spin.

'Laptops with certain batteries and PC Card combinations can, on occasion, generate an amazing amount of radio frequency across a wide spectrum,' says a spokesman for one of the US domestic carriers. 'The problem is in trying to identify the exact circumstances in which these phenomena can occur.

'Where you're seated in the 'plane could be a factor. If a passenger sits over the wing, for example, radio interference from his notebook could go out of the window and bounce off the jet's antenna. Yet, any other seat might be fine. Aircraft whose exteriors are made from composite materials, as opposed to all-metal, seem more at risk, as they don't reflect internal radio emissions as well.'

On the other hand, internally reflected radio waves could pose a problem if you're flying in a more modern aircraft. Unlike the elderly Boeings and their siblings, whose flaps and rudder are mostly operated mechanically, those on, for example, the European Airbus are controlled electronically by a wire running down the middle of the plane. Here, the potential for interference must be much greater.

The various carriers seem divided over exactly what constitutes a hazard, though, so pay careful heed to what the cabin staff have to say regarding the use of electronic equipment inflight. Study the airline magazine (usually tucked away, along with the sick-bag, in the pocket of the seat directly in front).

At the time of writing I had a copy of *Atlantica*, Icelandair's inflight magazine, in front of me in which it said that the company had banned portable telephones, together with radios, portable television sets, and similar. Perhaps surprisingly, heart pacemakers are included in this list of suspect electronics, too. Nevertheless, Icelandair kindly concedes that, should you be fitted with such a device, you'll most likely be permitted to keep it running for the duration of the flight.

Anyway, right there at the bottom of the list, alongside Walkmen and pocket calculators, are laptops and pocket computer games. These are acceptable, says the blurb, so long as you don't use them during takeoff and landing. Strictly *verboten*, however, at any time during the flight, are **radial mice** – mice that are connected to the serial port with a length of wire, as on the desktop PC.

In fact, as far as I'm aware all airlines now ban them. You're OK to use the trackerball variety, but the explanation for the ban on the other kind is that the wire acts as a kind of aerial. The longer it is, the greater the possibility of signals being amplified. So in other words, airlines fear that if you pull down one of your Windows menus or click on the 'Save' icon, you may send out a signal and cause the plane's undercarriage to drop, or make it jettison the contents of its fuel tanks over the Atlantic.

At the end of the day, however, I don't think anyone *really* believes that an Alicante-bound passenger playing 'Chuck Yeager: Test Pilot' on a notebook is suddenly going to cause the aircraft to behave like a sub-orbital rocket plane (anyone who's seen the film *The Right Stuff* and the way Chuck treats an F-105 will know what the consequences of that could be). It's just that in an industry as safety-conscious as the airlines, the watchword has got to be caution. No doubt in due course a sensible set of guidelines for safe onboard computer usage will be set down.

Beware the Arm-rest

Why? Because there's often a magnetic catch used in aircraft arm-rests to help keep them in the upright position when they're raised. Though the magnetism is unlikely to affect your laptop, it just might corrupt any floppy disks you have lying around.

Beware Exploding Ink Cartridges

'I used to carry a portable inkjet printer until the ink cartridge exploded during one flight,' says one unfortunate. 'It ruined the printer and made an awful mess of everything packed around it in my luggage.'

This was due, no doubt, to changes in air pressure within the aircraft cabin. This phenomenon causes aerosols and bottles of aftershave to leak, too. So in order to be on the safe side, if you must travel with a portable printer, it might be a good idea to pack its ink cartridge separately.

Flat Batteries

A plane isn't a good place to let your laptop's batteries run down. Where do you recharge? Here's a tale.

Back in 1991, *The San Francisco Chronicle* reported that business people in their droves, particularly on long-haul flights, were forsaking the pleasures of the inflight film and complimentary drinks in favour of spending the flight ensconced in the toilets. At first, cabin crew probably suspected a sudden, fatal heart-attack. However, on forcing open the door they discovered a much more terrible truth: flat batteries.

Apparently, under-powered executives were taking advantage of the shaver sockets in the aircraft toilets to recharge their laptop nickel cadmium batteries. Naturally enough, ni-cads being what they are, this was taking some time, much to the chagrin of other passengers – particularly those with weak bladders or who'd been hitting the inflight drinks in a big way.

It was reported that on one flight from San Francisco to Tokyo, virtually all the WCs were thus engaged. And if they weren't actually occupying the lavatories, what people were doing was booking seats at the back of the plane and then running back multiple extension leads. All this must have caused mayhem in the gangways as the duty-free trolleys became ensnared in the tangle of snaking cables.

Anyhow, one carrier decided enough was enough, sealed off its shaver sockets, and put up a terse notice explaining why. From that moment on, laptop owners were made to look like pariahs in the eyes of their fellow travelers – particularly those travelers who suffered from acute 5 o' clock shadow. They had to either resign themselves to designer stubble or learn to wet-shave. Nowadays, many aircraft shaver sockets will automatically shut down if used continuously for more than about five minutes, so it's not practical to use them for recharging.

But actually, there's no excuse for having flat batteries, even on long-haul flight. If you know you're going to be using your laptop continuously while flying, you should always take along a couple of spare, charged battery packs. There are, however, a couple of things you can do to help prolong the life of your battery.

1. Carrying extra batteries is an obvious one. Then again, you may be an insomniac doing a London to Sydney flight. This takes about 24 hours, which would mean, if you were intending to work all the time, you'd need about five spare batteries. Bear in mind, batteries aren't lightweight – five will amount to quite a weight.

2. Use a **RAM disk**, assuming your computer allows you to create one. A RAM disk emulates hard-disk storage. Here, you copy your programs and files into random access memory. This means that when your computer program is carrying out various functions, such as invoking the spellchecker or scrolling from one end of a document to the other, it accesses the data from the computer memory instead of having to go to the hard disk. This means there's less of a battery drain. But do remember that RAM is volatile: if the power goes, so does whatever you happen to be working on. With that in mind, also remember to copy your data from RAM back to the hard disk before switching off the laptop.

3. As I mentioned in Chapter 1, if you're using nickel cadmium or nickel metal hydride batteries, always ensure they are fully discharged before you recharge them again, otherwise they will hold progressively less and less power.

But failing all this, at the airport, before you set off, there are usually opportunities to top up your charge.

1. If you're a member of an airline club or are part of some frequent flyers' scheme, for example, then you're probably eligible to use the special lounges reserved by airlines for their VIP travelers. In here, as well as the complimentary bar and television, you'll find power sockets. Sometimes they're hidden on the underside of desks and tabletops. I assume you travel with an international power adapter as a matter of course. Take the opportunity to plug in and recharge while you down your gin and tonic, bearing in mind the Chapter 1 caveat about foreign power supplies.

But suppose you only travel Economy, or your chosen airline doesn't have its own lounge?

2. Look at the floor of the Departures Lounge. Does it have a carpet? If so, is the carpet clean and dust free? If it is, it follows that someone's been using a vacuum cleaner. Vacuum cleaners usually require external power supplies. Ergo, there's an AC socket nearby. Locate it, buy a cup of coffee, and plug in until your flight is called.

3. Look for one of those electric buggies that porters use to ferry suitcases around. If there's one sitting by itself, empty and stationary, the chances are it's recharging. This means there's an AC socket in the vicinity.

4. Look for table lamps. These days, more often than not, such items are hard-wired into the walls to stop passengers making off with them. However, if you're in an airport whose management has unfailing faith in human nature (Keflavik in Iceland is one), you could find they're simply plugged in. If so, unplug and recharge.

5. Ask a janitor or cleaner where the nearest AC socket is. He'll most likely tell you, but he'll probably want a tip as well.

The main point here is: don't be shy about plugging in and recharging. I have availed myself of airport electricity supplies in several airports worldwide, and have never yet incurred the wrath of the authorities. Nor has anyone ever asked me to pay for the electricity.

However, let's assume that, for whatever reason, disaster strikes while airborne and you find yourself power-less. It isn't quite the end of the world, but I must stress that what follows is a desperation remedy, only to be attempted when all other options are exhausted. I'm indebted to a commercial airline pilot who, by necessity, must remain anonymous.

'I'm a pilot who flies 747s for a major national carrier. Many of my colleagues bring their laptops to work with them and use them for extended periods during flight while off-duty (We carry double crews on the 12–16-hour flights).

'The problem of limited battery life is easily overcome by plugging your charger into a convenient socket that the air-craft cleaners use to plug in their specially modified vacuum cleaners. I say "specially modified" because an aircraft's elec-trical system is mostly 115 V AC at 400 Hz. A normal vacuum cleaner would probably suck the pile out of the carpet in the few seconds before it went into terminal meltdown.

'An "intelligent" charger, however, as found on all modern laptops, seems only to "see" the 115 V AC and appears to be quite happy to rectify 400 Hz to DC instead of the more common 50/60 Hz found at ground level. I mentioned this ruse to one of our Avionics engineers the other day and he was horrified. But the fact is that it is regularly done with no apparent ill-effects to chargers or laptops (or aircraft).

'The plug required is a US-type 2-pin or 3-pin, or an appropriate adapter. The sockets are generally on the side walls of the aircraft adjacent to vestibule areas, etc. Inevitably, the seats in these areas are the ones endowed with generous legroom and are therefore the most popular. The actual seat numbers will vary with aircraft type and configuration. You get one by checking in early and asking for one. In particular, try to check in ahead of couples with young children, as these are the people usually allocated such seats by the ground staff.

'Plugging in while airborne shouldn't be a problem. Since the seat is next to the window, it's most unlikely that any cabin crew member would even notice your little subterfuge, but a strategically placed newspaper, briefcase, sickbag, etc, should prove a satisfactory disguise.'

So there you have it from the horse's mouth, as it were. However, I myself would be extremely reluctant to do this without the benefit of at least three stripes on my sleeve. But as I said, it *is* the method of last resort.

Other Modes of Transport

Not everyone travels by air, of course. So what sort of problems might occur on other forms of transport, and how do you overcome them?

Ships

Ships are a fairly laptop-friendly way of traveling, with few reported problems, unless you try working on deck in a heavy swell. Salt spray and computer chips don't mix. Another possible danger area is the cigarette lighter if you're traveling in a small boat, such as a cabin cruiser. Unlike those in the cars that supply 12 volts, the aquatic variety often pump out 24 volts. This will fry something expecting 12 volts, such as a laptop. So make polite enquiries before you whip out your AC adapter. Otherwise, you're essentially in a floating hotel, with all of a hotel's amenities, including sensible power supplies, large writing desks and the like. But just bear in mind that in the event of hitting an iceberg or mine, portable computers are neither waterproof nor particularly buoyant.

Cars

Obviously don't try to drive and use the computer at the same time, but if you're a passenger, and the car's suspension is adequate, you can usually work in transit. Indeed, if the car has a cigarette lighter – and the majority do – you can use its socket for powering or recharging the computer. Most major manufacturers supply 12 volt converters for this very purpose. One note of caution, though. If the car is stationary, and its engine turned off, prolonged use of the laptop will have the same effect on the car battery as leaving the headlights switched on.

Trains

A bit of caution is required on trains, particularly if you're traveling standard class on a British train where the buffet car is in the centre, so people are always going up and down the central corridor, carrying – and sometimes spilling – drinks. Try to get a seat by the window to minimize the risk of your laptop being drenched in gin and tonic. If possible, too, try to get a seat where the windows have curtains or a shade. If you're plagued by sunlight reflecting back from your LCD screen, this will help cut it out.

In terms of power supply, a train is about as bad a place to get flat batteries as a plane. As in a plane, the lavatory shaver sockets will cut out after about five minutes, meaning you can't charge from there. On some trains, there are 110 volt outlets placed either under or beside the seats. With an appropriate adapter, it's usually possible to plug in.

But have a care. The internal power supply on trains, especially electric trains, is often susceptible to extremely violent surges. Not only that; sometimes it will cut out altogether, for no apparent reason. I'm sure everyone who's traveled by train has at one time or another experienced the lights going off or dimming as the train has entered a tunnel. Therefore, don't rely on the train's power alone, and *always* use a power surge protector.

The Delights of Customs and Immigration

So, you and your laptop have survived the journey, and now anticipate many successful hours of word processing and spreadsheeting together. You have, however, to clear one final hurdle before you can start: Customs and Immigration. Some countries are extremely narrow-minded when it comes to allowing computers over their borders, therefore it's best to be prepared beforehand. As a basic rule of thumb: if you can't import a bottle of whisky, you can't import a laptop, either.

Europe, the Americas and the Far East should pose no problems at all. Some of the more officious officials may want to see proof of purchase, receipts, and so on, to make sure you're not trying to import the thing into the country to sell it. In a few airports, particularly in the United States, you'll be required to switch on the computer to satisfy Security that there isn't a bomb inside. Otherwise, it should be plain sailing. But certain regimes in the Middle East and North Africa are extremely computer hostile. If you try to sneak one in, you risk confiscation or, in worst-case scenarios, long terms of imprisonment. So unless you're traveling on a diplomatic passport, don't even think about it.

Libya

Computers *per se* aren't actually illegal in Libya. In downtown Tripoli they are readily available, albeit at very unreasonable prices. What *is* illegal, though, is trying to import one. If they catch you at it, State Security will confiscate your laptop and issue you a receipt for it. The downside of this is that the receipt isn't redeemable upon exit. It's merely an official notification that they've confiscated an illegal import and that it will never be seen again. So tough luck.

Even if you fancy yourself as a bit of a James Bond, sneaking a computer in is fraught with difficulties. At the time of writing, Libya is under UN embargo, so getting in and out is somewhat complicated. Indeed, there are currently only two ways to enter the country. The first is by ferry from Malta. Unfortunately, all baggage is X-rayed as you leave the ship, so there's no way to get a computer in there. Or you could come in by road from Egypt or Tunisia. Naturally, your baggage is thoroughly searched and newspapers, radios, computers confiscated. However, if you hide your laptop under the carpet under the car seat they are most unlikely to find it. Then again, they might.

Tunisia

You'd think that, seeing as this country is now a popular holiday destination, they would have a rather liberal attitude towards hi-tech equipment. In fact, although they aren't so doctrinaire as the Libyans, Tunisian officials are nevertheless highly suspicious of portable computers. Yes, they will permit the casual import of laptops, but only after rigorous examination.

The first thing they'll do is ask you to switch the thing on in order that they can examine the contents of your hard disk. If they can't access a file by simply double-clicking on it, they'll delete it. On the other hand, they might just delete the whole hard disk as a matter of course. They will then try to placate you by pointing out that it's possible to replace the software very cheaply by buying it in Tunisia – it is, so long as you're happy with pirated versions.

If you meet an amenable customs official who is too busy to delete anything, or you do manage to sneak the computer in, you're not necessarily guaranteed an easy ride thereafter. Upon exit, you'll be searched again. If they find a laptop in your luggage, they will ask you both to prove that it belongs to you, and that you are authorized to export it.

The most hassle-free way of getting a laptop into Tunisia is to re-format the hard disk upon entry and obtain a customs clearance form. Then again, this can sometimes be self-defeating. Asking for paperwork makes them more interested in looking more closely at the computer.

Syria

Syria is a bit strange in that, although you can take a laptop in, modems are against the law. Therefore, any laptop containing a modem is theoretically forfeit on entry. However, unlike Libya, you will get it back upon exit. If you sneak a laptop/modem combination in and then try to make an international phone call, all hell can break loose. I am indebted to a British businessman for the following story. For obvious reasons, he must stay anonymous.

'All international phone lines are monitored. What is hilarious is that if you try to speak in, say, Dutch or Hungarian, a voice comes on the line saying, "Speak in English, I don't know this language." If you don't comply, then you are cut off.

'The situation is even more extreme when it comes to data communications. Fax machines have only become legal in Syria very recently – so long as you use them on a state registered fax line. You can therefore usually get away with plugging a modem into a fax line. But be careful. When I was last in Syria, I tried to do a modem transfer on a newly registered fax line. Within minutes, we had the line cut and a visit by leather jacket clad secret police. They were very polite and demanded to see our authorization for the fax. Luckily, by this time, I'd hidden my laptop and plugged the fax back in, so the police quickly disappeared, apparently satisfied. I really don't understand the paranoia about communications in Syria, but it is ubiquitous in the region.'

Ethiopia

And finally, from Robert Becker, a tale of Ethiopia.

'In Ethiopia you have to register your laptop on the way in. They may note its serial number on your passport on the page where your visa is. They then check again on exit, to make sure the laptop you're taking out is the same one you brought in.

'I ran into a problem once because I entered the country and was met at the airport by a representative of a high government official. We never went through customs. On the way out I had to tell several people the name of the high official in whose care I had been.'

* * *

So much for getting your laptop into the country. Now what are you going to do with it?

3: Phoning Home

Now we come to the section of the book where, by necessity, things become technical – but hopefully not overly so. Let me assure you: if you know how to wire a plug and use a word processor, then you already have more than enough technical competence to connect your laptop and modem to a foreign telephone system and dial out. It's simply a matter of mastering the basics and ignoring the jargon.

From Business Suite to Satellite

I'm assuming that you're using your laptop, not just for on-the-road note taking and the like, but also to communicate the fruits of your labors, either as fax or data, back home or to the office at regular intervals. What are the options here?

If you're a business traveler staying in a franchise hotel chain or in one of the better four or five star independents, it's becoming increasingly likely that the hotel will offer some sort of **business suite** as a matter of course. Usually, these suites include banks of PCs, fax machines, printers and, latterly, modems – for a price, naturally. So it's just a case of transferring a disk from your laptop to the hotel computer and then paying for use of those facilities. They'll often include the services of a secretary who will do all the legwork for you.

However, your particular hotel might not be so blessed. Maybe it is, but you don't want to pay the potentially extortionate business-suite rates. Or it could be that the material you want to transmit home is fairly sensitive. You therefore don't want the risk of prying eyes looking it over. You would prefer to send your faxes or e-mail directly from your bedroom. This means using the telephone line in your room – if you can access it.

Then, there's of course a third possibility. You're not staying in a hotel at all, but in a private house or apartment. Which means accessing the domestic telephone line. Or, if you're working from an overseas office, you'll have to connect through the office system. This could mean bypassing an unco-operative, aged switchboard.

The fourth possibility, an unlikely one in the telecommunications age, granted, is that there's no physical means of accessing the phone system either from the hotel, the home, or the office. Which means falling back on the public telephone system and maybe using a coin or credit card operated payphone.

Finally, there is the nightmare scenario. The country you're visiting has no telecommunications infrastructure whatsoever. Either it's been destroyed by civil or military insurrection, by natural disaster, or there's never been one in the first place. Whichever, your only options here are cellular telephone or satellite links.

Fortunately, in the majority of cases, the laptop-equipped overseas traveler is likely to be staying in a hotel. So I'll start here.

Connecting from a Hotel

If the hotel has a business suite and you can afford it, use it. If not, you're probably going to have to go in through the telephone system in your bedroom. Success is therefore largely dependent on two variables: (i) the ability of your modem to actually communicate over the foreign telephone line; and (ii) connecting it to that telephone line in the first place. Basically, assuming there's a socket, will your modem's plug fit?

In all likelihood, the answer is a resounding 'No.' For those who revel in such trivia (i.e. trainspotters and budding party bores) the standard British Telecom plug is called a BT631A. Unfortunately, it's only welcomed by sockets in New Zealand, Gibraltar, Malta, and a few remnants of the British Empire.

The nearest thing to a universal plug – the American **RJ-11** – is only universal in the USA, most of the Far East, Spain, Iran, Turkey, Pakistan, and a couple of Arab Emirates (which is perhaps surprising for a country that's got the world to accept the Big Mac and Coca Cola). This means you're going to do a bit of homework before you travel.

Having done so, you'll find that there are in fact over 30 different types of telephone plug worldwide. Even that bastion of mass conformity, the European Union, whose very existence is dedicated to similarly precise regulation, permits at least nine variations on the theme. Some of them appear almost identical to the UK and USA varieties. Others look more like those mains-powered mosquito killers or drill bits.

The obvious solution here, people will say, is buy a **telephone plug adapter**, corresponding to whatever country you happen to be visiting. Your native phone plug will fit directly into a socket at the back, just like an AC adapter. Telephone plug adapters are readily available from many branches of

Tandy, Radio Shack, and a number of computer and telephone peripheral stores. They are also sold by specialized outlets, such as TeleAdapt in the UK, USA and Australia and Power Express in the USA.

Except it isn't always that easy. The telephone systems in many hotels, for example – particularly the international chains – are often dictated by the nationality of the company that built them, rather than the host country's standard. To take but one case: Reykjavik's American-built Holiday Inn has US RJ-11 plugs throughout, while the German-built Saga Hotel, just half a mile up the road, has old-style German plugs. So is there any way of finding out beforehand?

Well, you could try ringing up the hotel yourself and asking. Sometimes you'll get lucky and find that the staff are technically aware. On other occasions, you won't. But in any case, beware. Imagine you get hold of a nervous receptionist. Imagine saying in a husky voice, 'I want you to pull out your plug and bring it to the telephone. I want you to describe it to me carefully. How many prongs has it got?' And so on. You might find yourself arrested when you eventually try to check in.

A better solution, therefore, might be to fax them pictures of various international telephone plugs, and bid them circle which one is theirs and fax the result back to you. To this end, you'll find a chart of international plugs at the front of this book which you can photocopy.

But suppose even this friendly approach yields no results? My basic advice is, wherever you're going, always to travel with an RJ-11 adapter, if nothing else. In many parts of the world, there's a better than even chance this will work. Otherwise, you're going to have to go in blind and take a series of international telephone plug adapters, crocodile clips, leads, and the like. I'll come to these in greater detail later on. However, before you splash out any money on one of these so-called 'Road Warrior' kits, think for a moment. There is a more obvious solution.

Connecting from a Hotel: The Fax

That's right – try to use the hotel's fax line. Today, virtually all hotels, wherever they happen to be in the world, have a fax machine of some description. In countries where telecommunications are notoriously bad, it's often the case that the fax line is the one, really clear line, while all the others fizz like a glass of Alka Seltzer. In addition:

1. You can be sure that the fax line offers a direct connection out of the building, so you don't have to bypass a switch-board.

2. You know that it's capable of handling modem data (as I said, all fax machines have modems in them).

3. Outside the UK, there is a strong likelihood that, unless the fax machine is physically hard-wired into the wall – and not many are – it will be fitted with a 'universal' RJ-11 plug.

All these factors would seem to make the fax machine an ideal first port of call. Except that the hotel management might not share your enthusiasm. How do you know that they'll allow you to plug your modem into their precious fax machine's socket?

Often, all you have to do is use your charm on the person in charge of the fax machine. If you're lacking in that department, try a bribe. Some hotels will happily allow you to plug your modem in and just charge you by per minute usage. An employee will stand by with a stopwatch. In some countries, however, the mere suggestion of usurping their fax seems on a par with asking to see their safe. In a few countries, it's illegal, and you may find yourself arrested for even bringing up the subject.

Just use your common sense. Does the fax machine handle all the room booking confirmations and, by extension, the hotel's income? If it does, then they're unlikely to allow some foreigner to mess around with it and potentially jeopardize their revenues. What you could do in such circumstances is offer to fit a **doubler socket**, to accommodate both your modem and the fax machine's plug. Then the two can operate in tandem, thus minimizing the risk of any of their incoming faxes going astray. But don't hold out any great hopes that they'll agree.

And if they don't agree, then you're going in through your hotel bedroom's telephone system. Here's where the fun starts.

I. The Executive Room with Phone Socket: An Overview
Although they might not have business suites, many of the better hotels offer what are generally called 'executive rooms.' These are usually distinguished from the common-or-garden variety by their enhanced fixtures and fittings, including a trouser press, an ice-making machine and a telephone in the bathroom. Also, and most important, they tend to have a **data socket**, usually alongside the standard telephone socket.

Sometimes, especially in the USA, these data sockets are built into the sides or the back of the telephone. They were originally put in to allow business people to plug in a fax machine and receive and send faxes in the privacy of their room. But of course, if a fax machine will plug in, so will a modem.

For the purposes of this chapter, I'll classify any room that offers a data socket as an executive room, whatever its room rate. If you're booked into one, congratulations. From a data transfer point of view, you couldn't have made a wiser choice. On the hardware side, all you need do is fit an adapter to your modem's jack. You might not even have to do this. Outside the UK, rooms that do offer data sockets are increasingly going over to the American RJ-11 standard. So if you're already equipped with such a plug, you're away.

Well maybe not quite. Before you can dial out, there may be just a few minor niggles that might muddy the otherwise clear waters.

1.   First, you might have to negotiate the hotel's switchboard before you can get an outside line.

2.   Slightly more problematical is the fact that modems are rather like many package tourists: they expect the rest of the world to speak their own language. By this, I mean they expect to hear their home country's **dial tone**, wherever they might be. But as anyone who's traveled abroad and used foreign telephones will attest, different countries can have their own unique tones, many of which will be completely unintelligible to a fresh-off-the-boat, visiting modem. In the UK alone, for instance, there are two. The first, from a digital exchange, is a low buzz, while the noise from an old-fashioned mechanical **Strowger** exchange sounds rather like a cat purring.

How does the modem know which to interpret as being a dial tone? The answer is, it doesn't. If the noise that comes back at it isn't immediately intelligible, it will simply respond with a terse 'NO DIALTONE' and then sit there and sulk. No go.

3. What sort of exchange are you dialing? As I said above, there are essentially two types: manual (or 'Strowger' – named after the undertaker who invented the system) and digital.

    A manual exchange can only be accessed using so-called **pulse dialing**. This dates from the days when all telephones had those rotary dials. Each number is represented by a series of clicks – generally speaking, one for the number 1; two for 2, and so on (Although in some countries, one pulse can mean 0, two can mean 1, and so on). Digital exchanges, on the other hand, can be accessed by both pulse *and* modern **tone dialing**. With tone dialing, which is increasingly becoming the norm these days, each number is represented by its own distinct tone.

    The modem has to be instructed beforehand by its controlling software whether to use pulse or tone dialing. If you try to dial a mechanical exchange by using tone dialing, it simply won't work.

4. Even if you've successfully dialled out and achieved a connection, some countries' telephone systems will still conspire against you. In Austria, Belgium, Czechoslovakia, and some parts of Germany, the local exchanges generate regular, high-frequency signals. These are intended to meter line usage for billing purposes, and are usually time-based. So, for instance, an international call which uses a unit's value more quickly will generate more pulses over a given time than a local call. And these pulses are often enough to cause the modem's error correction to over-compensate and eventually drop the line.

II. The Executive Room: Negotiating the Switchboard and Ignoring the Dial Tone

If your room has a direct line to the outside world and the dial tone coming from it is intelligible to your modem, you can use your laptop just as you would at home or in the office. If you're ringing your company's e-mail system or a commercial online service, the only adjustment you might have to make will be to prefix the telephone number with the appropriate international dialing code.

But what happens if you have to get through the hotel switchboard and then deal with a foreign dial tone? In both these cases, a simple modification to the modem's **initialization string** is required. The modem's *what*?

Sorry about this, but all communications software, be it fax or data, has to be able to tell the modem 'Wake up! Dial the number! Be quick about it!' It does this by prefixing the target modem's telephone number with a variety of different codes, each of which instructs the modem to carry out a specific function. And because different manufacturers' modems can respond in different ways, it's sometimes necessary to tailor a unique set of codes specific to a particular make of modem. Or, you might want to override the modem's default instructions. For example, by default, most modems won't respond to an incoming telephone call. However, by prefixing the telephone number with a special coded instruction, you can tell the modem to ignore its inbuilt programming and respond when called.

These codes – the so-called 'Hayes Code' (not to be confused with the US anti-pornography legislation of the 1930s and 40s) – are called the 'initialization string'.

To tell a Psion Dacom modem to sit up and pay attention and ready it for calling CIX in the UK, for example, you might typically prefix the telephone number with: **AT F10 M1 C1 DT**. It sounds like a knitting pattern doesn't it? Translated from the vernacular:

1.   AT means 'Wake up!' All modem initialization strings have to be prefixed with this, or none of the other commands will be accepted.

2.   F10 means 'Set the data transfer rate to 14 400 bytes per second' (the equivalent of telling a car to go at 70 mph instead of 30).

3.   M1 means 'keep your speaker volume on until you're connected.' This gives you an audible check that your modem is actually dialing, that the target modem is ringing (as opposed to being engaged or unobtainable) and that the target modem then answers.

4.   C1 means 'If you understand everything I've told you, say "OK".' If the modem doesn't, and you've made a mistake with the initialization string, it will say 'ERROR' instead.

5.   DT means 'When you dial, use tone dialing rather than pulse dialing.' I've explained the difference between the two above.

Long-winded, isn't it? Thankfully, these days we don't usually have to concern ourselves with any of this nonsense. In fact, if you normally use a modern communications package, like WinFax or WinCIM for CompuServe, you may never even have seen an initialization string. It will be hidden away somewhere, probably under a 'Configuration' sub-menu. Indeed, at installation the majority of these programs ask you what sort of modem you've got, and then automatically set the initialization string that works best for that modem. Thereafter, you can forget all about it.

But, when you travel abroad, the initialization string may require minor modifications. Exactly how you modify it depends on the package you're using. Usually, it's just a matter of clicking on the 'Communications' or 'Modem Settings' menu with the mouse, and then going through to a secondary menu called, more often than not, 'Configuration.'

Let's assume initially, however, that we're going in manually using a simple text-based **terminal program**, such as Telix. Think of a terminal program as being like an old fashioned MS-DOS word processor. In the bad old days, we all had to use such programs to contact bulletin boards and conferencing systems. Today, only a masochist would work this way. Nevertheless, by displaying the data in the raw, it will allow me to show a complete initialization string in action and explain what each element does.

OK. I want to dial the CIX conferencing system, which is based just outside London in the UK. Its number – the one I normally dial from my home in the UK – is 0181 296 1255. My local exchange is digital, so I use tone dialing. If I were doing this through a terminal program from my front room, the initialization string would be:

AT F10 M1 C1 DT 0181 296 1255 ^ M

In other words, it's the standard initialization string given above, suffixed with the standard telephone number. The additional ^M, by the way, is simply the command for 'Enter,' or carriage return.

However, let's assume I am now on holiday in sunny Ulan Bator in Mongolia, and I need to contact CIX from there. Fortunately, the equivalent of the Ulan Bator Hilton has furnished me with an executive room, complete with telephone socket. So I plug my modem in and go for it. There are just a few problems now left to surmount.

1.   Ulan Bator's exchange is mechanical, rather than digital, so I can't use my normal tone dialing.

2.   I have to negotiate the hotel's switchboard to get an outside line. This requires prefixing the normal telephone number with a 9.

3. Because I'm making an international call, after the 9, I also have to insert the code for an overseas call which, in this case, is 00, plus the UK code, which is 44, and then the normal CIX telephone number, minus the leading zero.

4. The Mongolian dial tone sounds like a New Age rock group tuning up. No way does the modem want to acknowledge it. 'NO DIALTONE,' it tells me, sulkily. I therefore have to amend the comms program to get it to tell the modem to ignore anything it hears from the telephone line and proceed normally.

This is what I dial:

AT X1 F10 M1 C1 DP 9, 00 44 181 296 1255 ˆM

You'll see it's much the same as the above, with the exception of three marked additions.

1. X1 means 'Don't bother listening out for your normal dial tone – dial out regardless.' It's usually a good idea to insert this code into your initialization string as a matter of course whenever you're traveling internationally. Inability to understand foreign dial tones is one of the major reasons why modems don't work when taken abroad.

2. DP is the command for pulse dial, as opposed to tone dialing.

3. Note the comma after the number 9, which is the number used to obtain an outside line from the hotel. If you were dialing manually with the bedside telephone, you'd normally have to pause after the 9 to allow the internal exchange to switch you through to the external line. This is what the comma does. As the initialization and dialing string is executed, it inserts a pause – usually of between

half a second and two seconds, depending on the modem – giving time for this changeover to take place.

III. The Executive Room: How to Cope with a Combination of Digital and Mechanical Exchanges

If everything's in order, your comms package will say 'OK' and dial out. A few seconds later the modem will connect to CIX in Great Britain. A complication can arise, however, if the hotel's exchange is digital but the country's telephone system is the old-style mechanical. This you overcome by inserting a DP – pulse dial command – immediately after the 9:

AT X1 F10 M1 C1 DT 9, DP 00 44 181 296 1255 ^M

Suppose the hotel's system is mechanical, but the country has gone digital? Then it doesn't matter. As I said above, pulse dialing will usually cope with both mechanical and digital exchanges. So the DP command in the initialization string should cover both eventualities.

I know it might sound unnecessarily complicated, but once the initialization string has been edited and saved, thereafter your modem and comms package should perform exactly as they do in the office back home. In other words it will be plug in and play. You'll only need to adjust the settings if you move to another location.

IV. The Executive Room: Dialling out with WinCIM and MacCIM

As I said, these days no-one of balanced mind uses a modem with a bog-standard terminal program. People use graphical-based commercial packages instead, which turn the whole comms business into a push-button affair. Let's take the example of WinCIM, the Windows-based communications package for CompuServe. The reason I choose this is that, outside the Internet, CompuServe is the world's largest commercial online system, and WinCIM the most popular software used for accessing it.

We're still in Ulan Bator, remember. This time, instead of ringing CIX, I want to use WinCIM for accessing the London CompuServe node, whose UK number is 0171 490 8881. Normally, of course, I'd try to contact a CompuServe node closer to Mongolia in order to save on international telecommunications charges, but this is just for demonstration purposes.

1. Having fired up WinCIM, go to the 'Session Settings' selection under the 'Special' menu (Fig. 1).

2. Click on 'Session Settings', which will take you into a section headed 'Setup Session Settings' (Fig. 2). Here, although there are a number of items, you actually just have to make two simple amendments. The first is to the telephone number. You'll see that I've put in the number

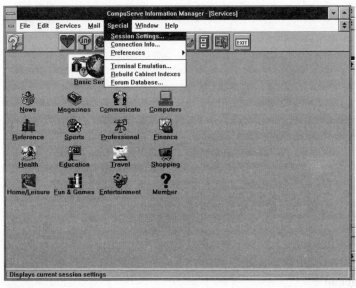

Fig. 1

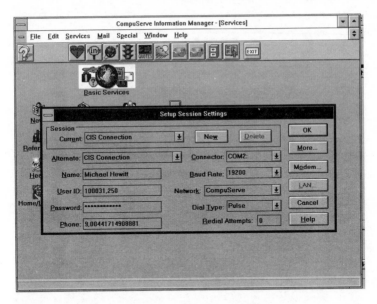

Fig. 2

9 to get an outside line, inserted the comma, and then prefixed the London CompuServe number with 00 and 44. The second change is to the box marked 'Dial Type', which I've reset to 'Pulse' from the original 'Tone'.

3. This done, I click on 'Modem', which takes me to a section called 'Modem Control Strings' (Fig. 3). Here, I simply add the X1 command – ignore the dial tone – to the 'Initialize' box, which contains the initialization string. This done, I click on OK. This takes me back to 'Session Settings' (Fig. 2) where I click on 'OK' again. This saves all the changes I've just made.

Now, the modem should ignore the Mongolian dial tone, get an external line, dial out to CompuServe in London using pulse dialing, and – hopefully – connect.

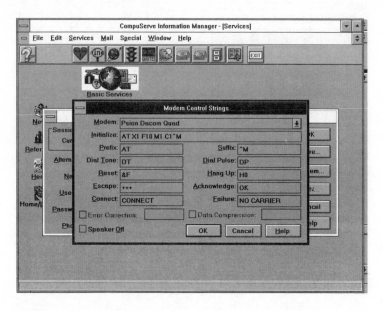

Fig. 3

MacCIM   Of course, let it not be thought that the only portable computers around are PC compatibles. The first Mac portable was doing the rounds several years before it was practical to put a GUI interface on an MS-DOS machine. The current generation of portable Macintoshes – the PowerBooks – are at least as powerful as their desktop counterparts. Indeed, thanks to their ease of use and excellent power management facilities, several companies have standardized on them for their on-the-road requirements.

Anyhow, just as WinCIM is the most popular PC-based communications package for CompuServe, so MacCIM is the most popular for Macintoshes. Its *modus operandi* is much the same as that of its Windows sibling.

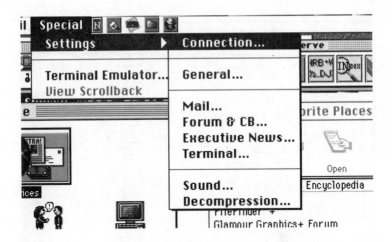

Fig. 4

1. Once you've started up MacCIM, go to 'Settings,' under the 'Special' menu, and then go to the 'Connection' option (Fig. 4).

2. This takes you to the 'Connection Settings' dialogue window (Fig. 5). Here, you'll probably need to change the telephone number, inserting a 9, a comma, the exit code, then your country's code. Also, change from tone to pulse dial if necessary. This done, click on 'Modem.'

3. Now you're in the 'Modem Settings' dialogue box (Fig. 6). The only change you'll have to make here is to insert an X1 into the modem's initialization string. This done, click on 'OK.'

As you can see, the process is almost identical to adjusting the session settings under WinCIM. Indeed, this follows for most comms programs, whether they be PC, Mac, UNIX, or whatever. The interface might be different, but the way you configure the modem is much the same in them all. Just look

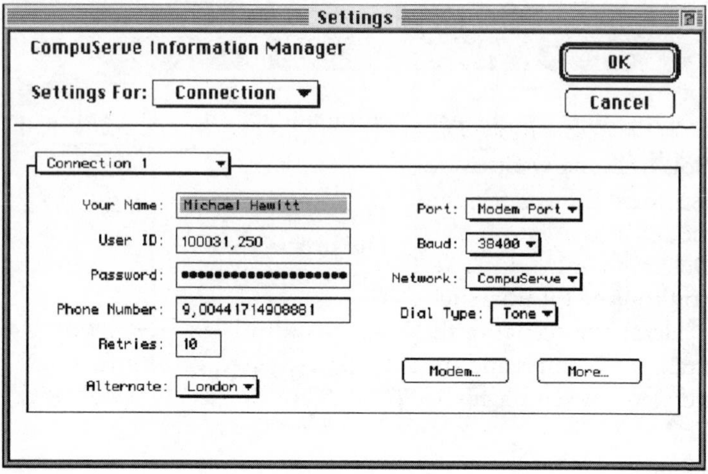

Settings

CompuServe Information Manager

OK

Cancel

Settings For: Connection ▼

Connection 1 ▼

Your Name: Michael Hewitt	Port: Modem Port ▼
User ID: 100031,250	Baud: 38400 ▼
Password: ••••••••••••••••••••••	Network: CompuServe ▼
Phone Number: 9,00441714908881	Dial Type: Tone ▼
Retries: 10	
Alternate: London ▼	Modem... More...

Fig. 5

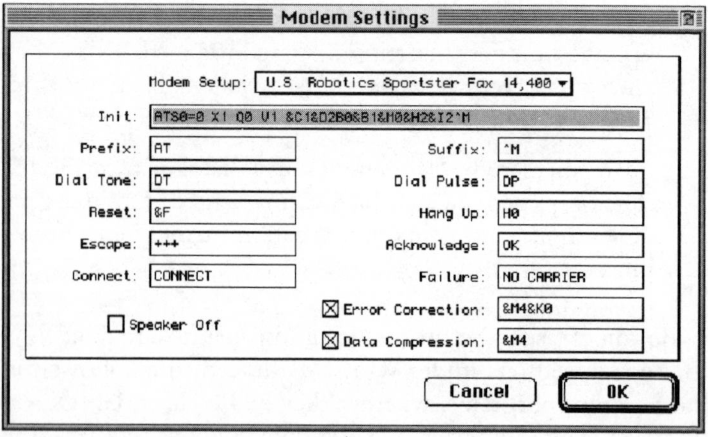

Modem Settings

Modem Setup: U.S. Robotics Sportster Fax 14,400 ▼

Init: ATS0=0 X1 Q0 V1 &C1&D2B0&B1&M0&H2&I2^M

Prefix: AT	Suffix: ^M
Dial Tone: DT	Dial Pulse: DP
Reset: &F	Hang Up: H0
Escape: +++	Acknowledge: OK
Connect: CONNECT	Failure: NO CARRIER
☐ Speaker Off	☒ Error Correction: &M4&K0
	☒ Data Compression: &M4

Cancel OK

Fig. 6

for a 'Configuration' or 'Session Settings' menu item, and take it from there.

V. The Executive Room: Dialing Out with WinFax

Not everyone wants to send e-mail, however. Many travelers use their laptops for sending and receiving faxes. Probably the most popular fax software used on portable computers is Delrina's WinFax Lite. I'll therefore go through the configuration routine for this, such as it is.

Here's the scenario, then. We're still in Ulan Bator, with its strange dial tones and mechanical exchange. This time round, we want to send a fax to a London number: 0171 467 3433. The telephone setup in the room is as before.

1. In the 'Phonebook,' the WinFax list of telephone numbers, amend the London number to 00 44 171 467 3433.

2. Choose 'Setup,' which you'll find under the 'Fax' menu. This takes you into the 'WinFax Setup' screen. Here, click on 'More'. This takes you to the 'Fax/ Modem Setup' screen (Fig. 7).

3. There are only two things to do here. By default, WinFax Lite *doesn't* wait for a recognizable dial tone. It will take what comes. Also, WinFax is automatically set for tone dialing. Therefore click in the 'Pulse Dial' box to enable pulse dialing. In the 'Dial Prefix' box, insert a 9, followed by a comma, to get you past the hotel exchange. And that's it. You don't have to put anything in the 'Init String' box to disable the dial tone detection box because, as I said, WinFax Lite isn't looking for one.

This done, you should be able to send faxes as normal.

```
┌─────────────────────────────────────────────────────────────┐
│                      Fax/Modem Setup                          │
├─────────────────────────────────────────────────────────────┤
│ ┌─Speaker Mode──────────────┐  ┌─Modem Setup───────────────┐ │
│ │ ○ Off                      │  │ ☒ Detect Busy Tone        │ │
│ │ ◉ On                       │  │ ☐ Detect Dial Tone        │ │
│ │ ○ Until Connected          │  │ ☒ Pulse Dial              │ │
│ │                            │                               │ │
│ ┌─Max Tx Rate──┐┌─Volume────┐  Dial Retries:  [0]           │ │
│ │ ◉ 9600       ││ ◉ Low     │  Dial Prefix:   [    ]        │ │
│ │ ○ 4800       ││ ○ Medium  │  Retry Time:    [60]  secs    │ │
│ │ ○ 2400       ││ ○ High    │  Init String:   [        ]    │ │
│ │                                                            │ │
│ ┌─Fax Header─────────────────────────────────────────────┐ │ │
│ │    Left: [                                            ] │ │ │
│ │  Center: [                                            ] │ │ │
│ │   Right: [                                            ] │ │ │
│ │                                                        │ │ │
│ │  Station Identifier: [                   ]  ┌────────┐ │ │ │
│ │     Sender Name:     [                   ]  │   OK   │ │ │ │
│ │                                             └────────┘ │ │ │
│ │                                             ┌────────┐ │ │ │
│ │                                             │ Cancel │ │ │ │
│ │                                             └────────┘ │ │ │
│ └────────────────────────────────────────────────────────┘ │
└─────────────────────────────────────────────────────────────┘
```

Fig. 7

VI. The Executive Room: Manual Dialing
The best laid plans of mice and men . . . . There will always be cases, for whatever reason, where your modem simply does not feel inclined to dial out through the hotel's telephone exchange. There is, however, an emergency fallback procedure: **manual dial.**

To do this, you'll need a **doubler** adapter. This is a twin socket adapter that allows both the modem and the telephone jacks to be plugged into the one telephone socket. What you're going to do here is dial out using the telephone itself, just as if you were making a normal voice call. Then, when the target modem squeals, you'll hit the Return key to initialize your comms software.

There are probably those of you who remember having to go through this sort of procedure with some of the early fax machines. Because they didn't have inbuilt diallers, they worked in tandem with the telephone. So you rang up the target fax, waited for it to respond, and when it did, you hit the 'Send' button and put the receiver down.

Essentially, there's no difference here. It just requires a little tinkering with the software. How much tinkering? That depends on the package you're using. Let's go back to the normal terminal program, as this is often the easiest to coax into life when dialing manually. The original initialization string setup for my Psion Dacom modem when dialing London from my fictitious Mongolian Hotel was, if you recall:

AT X1 F10 M1 C1 DP 9, 00 44 181 390 1255 ˆM

Of course, now, because I'm using the telephone to dial, it's the telephone itself that's coping with the dial tone, obtaining an outside line for me and calling my target modem. It does all the work for me. So I can dispense with all those elements in the initialization string that dealt with any of that. Let's just cut it down the middle, then:

AT X1 F10 M1 C1 D

There you go. I've sliced off everything that's superfluous, leaving just the rump. And in fact, that rump will suffice. Indeed, in most cases you can rely on the modem's internal default instructions. Then all you need to key in is:

AT X1 D

So the steps are:

1. Key the initialization string into your terminal screen.

2. Dial out on the telephone, just as if you were phoning home.

3. Let the phone ring. The modem at the other end will answer with its usual squeal.

4. When you hear the modem squealing, hit Return and put the telephone receiver down gently. Don't slam it down, or the modem might misinterpret it as being some sort of code.

5. Although you've put the receiver down, in fact you'll still be connected to the phone line via your modem. Therefore, it will be just as if you'd used the comms program to dial out in the normal manner. The two modems – yours and the target modem – will synchronize and then your respective comms programs will start talking to one another.

(N.B. When dialing manually, *always* insert an X1 into the initialization string. Most modems, by default, look out for a dial tone. But if you've connected manually, there will no longer be a dial tone to look out for – just a squealing from the target modem which could confuse your own unit.)

Simple isn't it?

Yes and no. It's simple when you're using a dumb terminal package. However, if you try to do the same with an elaborate Windows-based comms program, it will sometimes throw a tantrum. Why? Because some communications programs hand-hold the user so much that they can't conceive that the user would ever want to do anything as esoteric and independent as bypassing their internal comms modules.

So in some packages, for example, if when trying to log in manually you leave the telephone number box blank, they will beep angrily and refuse to proceed until it's filled in. The answer here is to fill it in – with 111, say, if you like. Or anything.

To be quite honest, it doesn't matter if there is a full telephone number in there.

If you dial manually, listen for the target modem and then start up your comms package, it will send out the telephone number as usual, and then – as usual – listen for a modem reaction. Which is exactly what it will get, because you've already contacted the modem by telephone. So just proceed as of step 4 above. The fact that you've previously sent a string of numbers should make no difference whatsoever.

Anyhow, I'm going to be talking about this in greater detail when, very shortly, I come to the subject of **acoustic couplers** in the next section. Essentially, connecting via an acoustic coupler requires an almost identical comms setup to connecting manually, as will be seen.

VII. The Executive Room: Line Noise

But suppose you've done all of the above, and yet still there are problems. Maybe, having contacted one another, your modem and the target modem act like a couple of quarreling grannies and simply refuse to talk. Or maybe you connect successfully at the beginning, but the line drops after a few seconds or in the middle of a download.

The most likely explanation here is **line noise**. There are two different varieties: natural and man-made.

Natural Line Noise Speaking very generally, the greater the distance between yourself and your contact, particularly if it's an international call, the greater the likelihood of interference. Third world exchanges can often be rather noisy. Also, neo-Stalinist, totalitarian regimes – if you can find any, these days – tend to offer a lousy phone service as a point of principle. Just holding a normal conversation can sound as if you've got a crossed line with a bee.

As time goes on, however, decent communications prevail, and satellite and digital microwave uplinks replace conventional landlines, so all this will become less of a problem. Where modernization has already happened, the difference in quality is dramatic. Singapore and other parts Far East, for example, now sound as if they're just down the road.

But where line noise is still a problem, you really are in the lap of the gods. Some modems are a lot better at coping with line noise than others. My own experience, for what it's worth, is that the Psion Dacom PDM 60 and the Pace Microlin PC Card modem are very good indeed and struggle on where many others would simply give up. But ask around. In particular, check out the computer magazines when they carry out comparative reviews of modems. The ability, or otherwise, to deal with a noisy line is usually one of the points tested.

Aside from that, there are a few other pointers:

1. Always use a modem that offers the most up-to-date error correction facilities, including V42 and LAP/M.

2. If, having connected at a high speed, you start to experience problems, try reconnecting at a lower speed. For instance, only the most naive optimist would attempt a 57400 bps connection from a third world payphone. Maybe 9600 bps, or 300 bps, would give better results.

3. Always use an error correction protocol such as Z Modem when uploading or downloading files. With Z Modem, if the line is dropped and the file transfer interrupted, you can reconnect later on and carry on with the download from the point at which you were cut off.

4. If you have no joy with your data transfer during the day, try again very late at night or in the early hours of the morning when there are fewer people using the phone network. This can make a dramatic difference in line quality. There aren't as many subscribers competing for the bandwidth, and there's less chance of interference from crossed lines.

Man-made Line Noise   This type of noise, alluded to above, is only really a problem in Austria, Belgium, some parts of Germany, and a few former 'Eastern Bloc' countries. This is deliberately created line noise made up of **high-frequency/ high-pulse signals**. It manifests itself as that seemingly random 'beep . . . beep' sound. There are more beeps on a long-distance call than a local call. Sometimes, the modem will interpret them as line noise and try to compensate, thereby slowing down data transfers. Sometimes, it will give up altogether and drop the connection.

If you're staying in a hotel, these tones might not be a problem as the internal exchange will often filter them out. If it doesn't, however, you can buy your own filter from companies like TeleAdapt and Power Point. These are simple in-line devices that connect between the modem and the phone socket to filter out the extraneous frequencies. They are completely transparent to the user, and don't require a battery or external power.

* * *

So much for the executive room, or any hotel room with a telephone socket. But what happens if, horror of horrors, you enter the room and find that, apparently, there isn't a telephone socket? Read on.

4: Hard-wiring and Acoustic Couplers

N.B. Before you attempt any of the techniques described in this chapter, I would strongly recommend that you carry out a few trial runs on your home or office telephone system first. By gaining confidence there, it won't seem nearly so daunting when you eventually get out in the field. I will admit that when I first had to connect my modem into a foreign telephone system, I *did* find the whole thing rather daunting. (Then again, at first, I found wiring a plug equally so.) With practice, it becomes second nature. So practise at home where the phone bills aren't as high. What follows might seem complicated on paper. It isn't nearly as complicated when you get used to it.

If you can't connect through a telephone socket, you have two choices: hard-wiring or an acoustic coupler. Each method has its aficionados. Some people swear by acoustic couplers, others swear at them. In this chapter, I'll look at the options. Ultimately, it's up to you to decide.

The Road Warrior Kit

Before I go any further, I'm first of all going to list the equipment you'll need for connecting your modem to the telephone system. There are lots of different ways to splice yourself in, depending on what sort of system it is and how it's built. Which means that, if you don't know what you're going to encounter, it's wise to travel with the appropriate equipment to cover every eventuality. Hopefully, it won't come to this

because there will be a socket, but you never know. And because you never know, the seasoned laptop equipped traveler is always prepared.

All the following items can be sourced separately, or else they can be purchased as complete kits. For example, TeleAdapt in the UK, USA, and Australia and A R Industries in the USA call theirs 'Road Warrior' kits. Usually, all the bits and pieces fit into a small black bag. If you wander around with one, it often looks as if you're a doctor, come to take someone's appendix out. Anyway, the constituent elements should include:

1. A collection of telephone plug adapters, including a US RJ-11 and some of the more common European types.

2. A modular duplex jack. This is the doubler adapter I was talking about earlier that allows the phone and the modem to be plugged into the same socket.

3. A small torch. If you're going to poke around someone's telephone system, there will be all sorts of dark nooks and crannies to search.

4. A selection of small screwdrivers, for use with standard cross-heads and Phillips heads.

5. Crocodile clips. Or 'alligator clips', as they're called in the USA. These come in pairs which clip on to naked phone wires and terminate in an RJ-11 plug, that goes directly into the modem.

6. A penknife, for scraping insulation off telephone wires.

7. A small pair of pliers.

8. A line-tester. These are normally small plastic devices with an integral diode. You attach the crocodile clips to the line tester. Its diode then glows either red, green, or yellow, depending on the polarity of the telephone line you're attempting to hook into.

9. A telephone line extension cord. The socket may be some way from where your computer is positioned.

10. A telephone line surge protector. Mentioned earlier. This stops sudden electrical surges, such as those caused by lightning strikes, frying your modem.

11. A roll of insulated electrical tape for holding things together that don't belong together naturally.

12. A telephone handset connector. Mentioned above. For connecting through the telephone handset's RJ-11 socket.

13. An acoustic coupler. For when all else fails, and you're forced to use the telephone as nature intended.

14. A small corkscrew. You may want to celebrate with a decent bottle of wine after having made a successful connection.

Now let's get back to the hotel bedroom.

Finding the Hidden Socket

So, you're in your hotel room but, nice though it is, you feel that it lacks a certain something. To be specific, it lacks a telephone socket. Or does it?

Look around before you start to despair. Take the telephone wire and follow it back. Where does it terminate? Often, there's a very good chance that the hotel has arranged things such that there actually *is* a socket, but it's hidden away behind some fixture or fitting which the management feel you will be too lazy, or too unadventurous, to shift.

In the Grand Hotel Excelsior in Viareggio, in Italy, for example, the socket is behind a heavy wooden bedside table. In the Sheraton Skyline Hotel, just outside Heathrow Airport, the socket is tucked away behind the bedhead in some of the rooms. Without much undue strain, it's very easy to shift this to one side and then gain access. Indeed, internationally, the bedhead is often a favored phone plug impediment. Try there first. In other hotels – particularly those swish ones with a wall-mounted telephone in the bathroom – the phone can simply lifted off the wall-bracket, revealing a socket underneath.

But suppose the wire simply disappears into the wall? All may not be lost. Check the point of entry. Unless they've physically drilled a hole in the plaster – and this is very unlikely – very often, there's simply a plastic or metal plate at skirting board level, secured by a couple of screws. Remove it and, if you're lucky, you'll find a conventional telephone socket within. Proceed as with the executive room from this point, but do remember to replace the plate.

What happens, though, if the phone cable doesn't just disappear into the wall, it's engulfed by it? Its point of entry is buried beneath layers of marble fascia and oak panelling. This is unlikely to be a problem in the US, where today most hotels are modem friendly. But in Europe – particularly in some of the snootier five star hotels – it seems to be company policy, presumably to prevent the well-heeled guests making off with the phone as a souvenir of their stay.

There are two possible courses of action here. First, you can literally tear the furnishings apart in order to try to find a usable socket. However, the only way to do this without being arrested for criminal damage is to pretend to be a member of a heavy metal rock group with an angst problem. Unfortunately, this also entails throwing the television set out of the window, filling the bath with tequila, and inviting groupies up to the room.

Failing that, then, try looking at the telephone handset.

In Through the Handset: I

Telephone handsets, fortunately, tend not to be as collectible as the phones themselves. It's therefore quite possible that yours is detachable from the main unit. If so, you can often connect your modem via the handset's socket. This is usually RJ-11 size, and sits at the bottom of the handset. There are devices, variously called a **Konnex** (a trademark of Unlimited Systems), a **TeleSwitch** from TeleAdapt, or whatever, that allow you to do this, available from specialist and computer peripheral stores.

The handset connector is usually powered by an internal 9 volt battery, though there are some mains powered versions. It sits between the modem and the phone. One wire runs into the switch from the modem, the other runs from the modem to the handset socket. Once everything is plugged together, you should then be able to use the modem just as if it were hard-wired directly to phone line itself.

Sometimes, however, the internal workings of the telephone conspire to prevent this. Or maybe you've drawn the short straw and been booked into a hotel which has suffered in the past from a plague of telephone handset collectors. So to deter future guests from carrying out such trophy hunting, the management has ensured that not only is the phone hard-wired into the wall, but the handset is hardwired very firmly into the phone.

Now what?

In Through the Handset: II

Can you unscrew the handset's mouthpiece, or will it somehow prise off? Of course, avoid causing any permanent damage to the hotel's equipment, so try each method carefully. Assuming you succeed, the telephone's microphone will pop out, and you should see two silver contacts at the base. The plan of action now is as follows:

1. Attach your red and green crocodile clips, one to each contact. It doesn't really matter which goes on which.

2. Put the receiver down and connect the cable from the crocodile clips into the modem. Then fire up your comms software as usual.

3. When you're ready to dial, simply pick up the telephone handset as if you were using the phone normally, and then activate your comms software as described above (disable dial tone detection, dial 9 for an outside line, etc). It *should* work just as if you were connecting in the normal way through a socket. However, before you go dialling an international number, try ringing somewhere local instead in order to test the connection. Preferably something inanimate like the Speaking Clock, that won't object to a modem squealing down the line at it. If everything is OK, your modem will dial out, make the connection, and the next thing you'll hear will be the Speaking Clock itself.

This proves that the connection works OK. Now dial your fax or modem number.

In Through the Handset: III

It could be, however, that going through the telephone handset in this way results in a certain amount of line interference. If so, you might try another method: go directly into the telephone itself. This is slightly more complicated and success depends largely on whether or not the telephone will come apart, and whether you actually want to take it apart. If you've got no moral qualms here, proceed as follows.

1. Remove the telephone's plastic case. This is usually secured to the telephone by four or more Phillips screws in the base. Once they're removed, a good tug usually detaches the case.

2. Look for the telephone's transformer. This will be the piece of heavy metal with a myriad of wires running out of it. Have a care, though: the thing will be live, albeit without any life-threatening voltages.

3. Locate the red and green wires running from the transformer, and attach the red and green crocodile clips.

4. Screw everything back together, or stick it together temporarily using electrical insulation tape.

5. Proceed as normal. Attach the wire from the crocodile clips to the modem, and then fire up the comms software. Remember to test the connection by dialling a local number first. If all is OK, you'll connect.

Long-winded? Overly technical? Yes, I agree. If you don't want to take the telephone apart and gain access through the unit, what are the alternatives?

Hard-wiring and Wire Tapping: The Legalities

You have two courses of action. You can either use an acoustic coupler, as I'll explain later on, or try to hard-wire your modem directly into the telephone system via the junction box or through the wall. The first is the easiest solution, but might not produce the best results. The second is surest in terms of guaranteeing line-quality and data integrity, but can be somewhat fiddly. Not difficult, just something of a bind. There is, however, another aspect to taking a telephone system apart and then hard-wiring: is it legal?

Technically, no. In the UK, for example, if a BT engineer were to walk in on you in flagranté with a pair of crocodile clips, he would be well within his rights to have your line disconnected. In the USA, a Federal Communications Commission (FCC) ruling insists that you contact the telephone company before attaching anything vaguely exotic to the line. In a hotel, if the management sees you've dismantled their phone system, they would be well within their rights to have you charged with criminal damage.

In reality, though, no one cares. BT engineers routinely find those red-stickered modems and all sorts of odds and ends plugged into the system without kicking up a fuss. In the USA, though the FCC does require advance notice before you plug a modem in, no one bothers. Who would try to enforce the law, anyway? And sure, hotel management could kick up a fuss if you unscrewed their telephone sockets, just as they could theoretically charge you with petty larceny if you walk off with one of their towels, but they just don't.

No, the biggest problem, as I said, is the hassle.

Hard-wiring: Method I

So, you've traced the telephone wire back to the skirting board, or wherever, but have discovered that there isn't actually a

socket in there. All you can find are bare wires. Sometimes there are just two or three. On other occasions, it looks like the output from a spaghetti factory on overtime. Don't be disheartened. Reach for your kit of parts, and proceed cheerfully.

The first thing to realize is that it really doesn't matter how many wires there are. Only two of them are going to be connected to the exchange or switchboard. The trick is to identify which two. Here is where the line-tester comes in. Most line-testers are about four inches long, and terminated by an RJ-11 plug. They are usually connected, by a socket coupler, to a pair of crocodile clips. The *modus operandi* seems complicated on paper, but I can assure you it is actually quite straightforward:

1. Fortify yourself with a strong drink, and then set to with a purpose.

2. From the jumble of wires, select two – any two – and attach one crocodile clip to each. If the wires are coated

in insulation material, you'll probably have to take your penknife and scrape this off first in order to get a decent connection.

3. If, having attached the line-tester, you get no result, mark the redundant wires with something like insulating tape, and move on to the next set.

4. If, by a stroke of luck, you select the right pair first time, the LED diode in the line tester will glow green. If you get a red light, it means you've got the right pair, but the wires are reversed.

    Beware a yellow light. A yellow light means there's AC current present on the line. If this happens, disconnect everything immediately, unless you want to get electrocuted.

5. It may sound long-winded, but by a logical process of elimination you'll eventually arrive at the correct pair of wires. Once you have, check the connection, just as before. Do this by removing the line-tester and plugging the phone into the socket coupler. Then dial a number, any number. Call room service, for instance, and order a pizza. If everything's functioning as it should, you'll get through. Once the line has been checked in this way, take out the phone and plug the modem in. Then proceed as above with initialization strings, commas, and the rest. Pausing first, of course, to consume your recently arrrived pizza.

Hard-wiring: Method II

The phone and its handset are an inseparable partnership – you must have shot an albatross recently. You can't go in through the handset. The telephone is one of those moulded plastic varieties, held together with specialized flanges and nuts. You could try taking it apart, but you sure as hell wouldn't be able to put it back together again. So that rules out going in through the transformer. Furthermore, the phone cable doesn't just disappear into the wall, its point of entry is buried beneath layers of marble fascia and oak panelling. Therefore, there isn't a skirting board panel to unscrew.

The solution? The wire leading from the telephone.

Using a very sharp penknife or razor blade, *carefully* make a C-shaped incision in the wire's insulation. Don't cut too hard, or you'll cut all the way through the wire and disconnect yourself, which will no doubt irritate the hotel greatly. Rather, just cut deep enough to make a small flap. Having done so, peel this back to reveal the individual wires within. Carefully pull them loose. Having identified which is which, proceed as above.

Isn't There an Easier Way?

It could be that you've tried everything above – in through a normal socket, the handset, the transformer, and the raw wires – but the telephone system still doesn't want to play. It could be that the hotel's PABX telephone exchange system and your modem are simply mutually inimical. Fact: there are telephone systems that are genuinely modem-hostile.

On the other hand, it could be that you don't want to have to start acting like some third-rate secret agent, performing specialized wire-taps. I can understand this. In both scenarios, therefore, you'll have to fall back on that old standby, the acoustic coupler.

Coupling Acoustically

Back in the low-tech days, an acoustic coupler was the only way of connecting a modem to the telephone system. It might be recalled that years ago, phones were hard-wired and few modems connected at speeds much above 300 bps. Indeed, there were few modems, and even fewer people with the technical and practical know-how to tinker with the wiring and connect them up directly. So an acoustic coupler was really the only practical method.

What is it exactly? An acoustic coupler consists of a loud-speaker and microphone combination that you place against the microphone and loudspeaker on the handset. A cable runs from these and plugs into the modem's line jack. So in other words, the signals from the modem are fed through the telephone handset, just like your voice.

The first such beasts came in briefcases and consisted of two large rubber suction-cups into which the handset was firmly squeezed and secured. The idea was that this arrangement minimized the likelihood of extraneous noise interfering with the connection. Today, however, miniaturization has triumphed. Most modem acoustic couplers look like squashed Walkman headphones or some variety of weird telephonic bondage gear.

Some of the more advanced models, such as the Telefast from TeleAdapt are much more substantial beasts. The TeleFast has the appearance of a complementary telephone handset. Powered by a 9 volt battery, it has a volume control to match the various telephone line conditions, and a series of rubber 'vibration isolation pods' at each end to dampen interference from ambient noises. Using one of these, you can usually achieve line speeds of up to 24 000 bps, but that really is pushing it. Normally, the best speed you'll get out of a standard acoustic coupler is around 2400 bps on data and maybe 4800 bps for fax. (At 4800 bps, just one A4 fax page is going to take at least a minute to go down the line. Bear this in mind if you're paying international charges *and* a hotel surcharge.) Personally, I tend to aim for 9600 bps and think myself lucky if I get 300 bps.

In the last paragraph, I assumed that the telephone was functioning properly. That is the crux of the matter. Your communications can only be as good as the handset to which your coupler is connected. With modern telephones, there shouldn't be too many problems, aside from the usual difficulties with line noise. However, if you find yourself in a room with one of those ancient Bell devices, it's conceivable things may go awry. Also, if there's a lot of ambient noise about – a band outside your bedroom window, for example – you'll find that could interfere with the data transmission. So how do you maximize your chances of coupling acoustically?

1.   If the telephone is one of those old, bakelite models or a 1970s' 'Trimphone,' it's probable that the speaker and microphone are of the carbon granule variety. If you ever have occasion to open one up and empty it, you'd find what looks amazingly like the contents of an ash tray. Over time, these granules can eventually clump together, impairing sound quality, which in turn adversely affects data transmission. So before use, tap the handset very lightly to separate them. Don't go overboard – just a little knock. Also, for whatever reason, telephones with carbon microphones seem to work better when used at the normal speaking angle, i.e. as if they were cradled against your ear. Try not to leave the receivers lying on their backs.

2.   Sometimes, the speaker and microphone in the coupler can be adversely affected by adjacent electronic components. These could be anything from the bedside lamp, the clock radio, or even the telephone itself. Therefore where possible place the handset/coupler combination in an area by itself.

3.   If external vibration is a problem – someone next-door is bouncing on a pogo stick or there are heavy lorries rumbling on the street outside – it's often a good idea to dangle the handset/coupler combination in mid-air during transmission.

4. If your coupler does not have its own sound insulation the best solution is to cover the handset/coupler combination with bedclothes and pillows. This should provide sufficient soundproofing to give a decent connection.

5. Ensure that the coupler's speaker is attached to the handset's microphone, and its microphone is attached to the handset's speaker. Many people get these connected the wrong way round, which effectively means the modem is 'deaf.' On most acoustic couplers, the microphone and speaker elements are clearly labeled, so there should be no confusion. However, on some of the more basic squashed Walkman types, you're expected to work it out for yourself. To do this, key ATDT12345 into your terminal program, hit Return, and then place your ear to what you imagine to be the coupler's speaker. If you *don't* hear the number dialling out, you're obviously listening in at the wrong end. Change over and try again.

6. Set the connection speed in your comms software. As I said, how fast you can go depends on both the quality of the modem and that of the telephone line. Don't be too ambitious, particularly if you're making an international call.

7. Once you're all plugged together and muffled, there are two courses of action. In the first instance, I'm assuming your telephone is of the tone dialling variety.

   (i) If you're using a conventional terminal package such as Telix or Window's Terminal, key the string ATX1DT, followed by the phone number. For instance, if I were dialling the London CompuServe node from my own home, I'd key in ATX1DT01714908881 and hit Return. (The insertion of X1, as I mentioned above, is simply a precaution, telling the modem to ignore the absence of a dial tone.) Then, the modem tone dials and feeds the tones via the coupler, through the handset. Thereupon, it should ring out as normal and connect.

(ii) It didn't? OK, there could be two problems here. Either your telephone system is of the old mechanical variety and doesn't respond to tone dialling, or the telephone unit itself, or the switchboard, is just playing hard to get. Don't worry. Key in the string ATX1DT (or you can follow it with the number, as well – it won't make any difference; see below) and then dial out manually using the telephone's keypad. Then wait.

8.   In both the above cases, you'll hear the dialling action – either rotary or touch-tone – then you'll hear the modem at the other end ringing. After a couple of rings it will start to squeal. At this point, hit Return. Thereupon, your modem and the target modem should negotiate their protocols and you will be in business just as if you'd connected conventionally.

N.B. I said that, when dialling manually, you could suffix the normal ATX1DT initialization string with your usual telephone number. It's worth mentioning this, because there's a common misconception that if you do so, you'll somehow sever the connection or confuse the target modem. So many people delete the telephone number or leave it out. In fact, it doesn't make a blind bit of difference. When the target modem squeals at your modem, it's basically saying 'Please exchange protocols with me.' Then it sits and waits, usually up to 30 seconds or so, for those protocols to be exchanged. If, in the meantime, you squirt a telephone number at the thing, it will simply ignore it. Indeed, you can speak loving endearments down the line, too, or breathe heavily. It will also ignore those. The only thing it will respond to, either positively or negatively, is an electronic signal from your modem.

Acoustic Couplers and Offline Readers

Surprisingly, the majority of acoustic coupler manufacturers automatically assume you're using a simple terminal package as described above, and don't bother to describe the device's operation when working with an offline reader, such as OzCIS for CompuServe, or with a fax package like WinFax. This isn't because there's anything particularly complicated about the process. Actually, connecting acoustically using a fax or offline reader package is as near as dammit like dialling out manually when you're hard-wired. I'll give three simple examples.

Ameol

Ameol is the standard Windows-based offline reader for the UK's CIX conferencing system. It dials up CIX, negotiates the modem protocol, uploads any mail or messages you have waiting, downloads mail and messages that are waiting for you, and finally disconnects. Then you can read everything offline, which means you're not running up a huge bill or connect-time charges.

Anyway, Ameol responds very positively to an acoustic coupler. Few, if any modifications are required to the usual setup.

1. Once booted up, click on the 'Menu' and then choose 'Communications.' This takes you to the 'Communications Settings' window (Fig. 8). Here, decrease the baud rate to something realistic, like 9600 bps – less if you're using a more primitive acoustic coupler.

2. Where necessary, amend the telephone number. For example, if you're going out through a hotel switchboard that requires the number 9 for an outside line, the modified CIX number would be 9,01813901255. Plus the usual international codes if you're dialling from abroad.

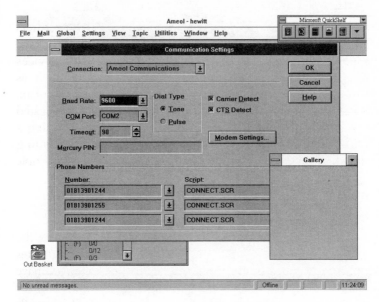

Fig. 8

3. Leave the 'Dial Type' set at 'Tone.' You can't pulse dial through an acoustic coupler. If you're using a pulse dial phone, you're going to have to dial out manually. This won't make any difference, though.

4. It might be a good idea also to amend the Timeout setting. This is the time that Ameol will wait for CIX to respond. If it doesn't get a response within the given time, it will drop the line and report back an error message. By default this is set to a generous 60 seconds which, under normal circumstances, is more than enough. However, I've sometimes found that it's wise to up this to around 90 seconds over some international lines.

5. This done, click on the 'Modem Settings' button which takes you, not surprisingly, to the 'Modem Settings' window (Fig. 9). Here, insert an X1 into the modem's initiali-

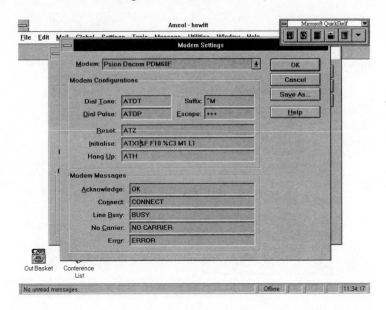

Fig. 9

zation string and hit Return. This returns you to the 'Communications Setup' window. Hit Return again, and you're in business.

6. At this point, dial out as described above. If it's a touch-tone telephone, then clicking on the Ameol telephone icon should dial through and connect in the normal manner. If it isn't a touch-tone unit, dial manually, wait for the target modem to start squealing, and then fire up Ameol. Once done, the software should behave exactly as it does at home or in the office, albeit a little more slowly.

WinFax Lite
Again, there is very little to this package. Indeed, the setup is exactly the same as with manual dialling. In other words,

check that the boxes for Detect Dial Tone and Pulse Dial are disabled. And, if you're dialling out through a switchboard that requires you to insert a number – a 9, for example – in order to get an outside line, put 9, in the Init String box.

WinCIM
WinCIM is the standard CompuServe front-end software. Like Ameol, it requires very few modifications.

1. Look under Special in the opening window and click on Session Settings. This takes you to the dialogue box.

2. Create a new session setting specifically for your acoustic coupler. You do this by clicking on the box marked 'New.' This brings up a 'New Session Name' dialogue box. Call it acoustic, or something equally memorable, and then click on OK, or hit Return. This takes you back to the Session Settings box.

3. In Fig. 10 you'll see that I've amended the telephone number, prefixing it with a 9 and a comma. This, of course, is to enable the modem to navigate past the switchboard. Also, I've set the communications speed to a more realistic 2400 bps. Some acoustic couplers can do better than this, most can't. However, if you're logging on to CompuServe from somewhere extremely exotic, a 2400 bps connection is often the best you can get, even when going in through the telephone socket in the usual way.

4. In Fig. 10, I've also opened up the modem settings dialogue box. Not surprisingly, this is done by clicking on 'Modem.' Here, the only change I've made is to insert an X1 – ignore dial tone – into the initialization string.

5. Click on OK, or hit Return, and your Session Settings are saved.

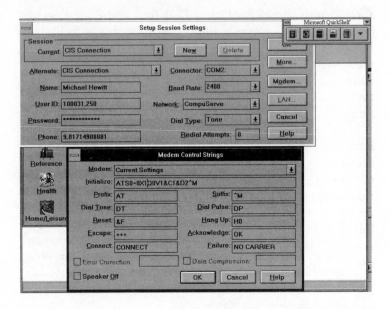

Fig. 10

6. Thereafter, attach the coupler to the telephone handset. Then fire up WinCIM in the usual way by clicking on the telephone icon. If the phone allows you to send tones through to obtain the number, the program should dial out and connect in the usual way. If not, you'll have to dial manually. When you hear the modem at the other end squealing, *then* click on the telephone icon.

As I said, some people love acoustic couplers, some people hate them. At worst, they won't work at all. At best, however, they can provide a connection almost the equal of that through a telephone plug or hard-wired line. It's a case of trial and error.

Cutting the Costs

Let's assume congratulations are in order, and you have successfully negotiated the hotel's telephone system and made a connection. There is, unfortunately, one niggling little afterthought which might cloud your otherwise well-deserved triumph. You actually have to pay for the call.

Hotel telephone surcharges are often as extortionate as hotel laundry bills. In just the same way that they can charge you a dollar per sock, so they'll slap surcharges of anything up to 66% on telephone bills. If you have to make a lot of international calls – fax connections, say – you can sometimes end up with a phone bill that exceeds the room rate and mini-bar bill combined. Even local calls, to the local CompuServe node, for example, can soon add up. So is there any way you can prevent them from lining their coffers at your expense?

Fortunately, yes. There are three ways. The first is to use a private **800 number**. The second is to use an international **telephone charge card**. The third is an international **call-back service**. Although the last two will require you to hand over an annual or monthly subscription, if you know you're going to be running up hefty international or long distance phone bills, they can more than pay for themselves over a period of time.

800 Numbers

Only of use if you're in the USA, unfortunately. A private 800 number that connects to your company's modems is often cheaper than a telephone charge card. You can get one for about $25 per month, plus $0.25 per minute tariff. Call up your local telecommunications company to check this out.

International Charge Cards

International charge cards work in most countries of the world. You phone a local node, usually a freephone number, and are connected via that node to an international line. Essentially, the *modus operandi* is much the same as for the Internet, which I described in the introduction. It's a piggyback system: one on top of the other.

Anyway, there are a number of companies offering such charge cards, all of them working in co-operation with international telecommunications companies. In the UK, for instance, there's World Telecom, while in the USA, AT&T are probably the best known. In both cases, savings of up to 30% are offered on standard international calls. If you're making those calls from a hotel, the savings of course can be much more. As an added bonus, when you're back home, many companies allow you to make free local telephone calls of up to two minutes.

When you sign up, you're given a list of dialup sites worldwide, your own personal registration number, and a unique PIN number. To use the card, you dial whichever site happens to be closest to you at the time. Thereupon, the recorded voice of an operator answers, and invites you to enter your registration number and your PIN number using the telephone's keypad. This you key in. Finally, when the system has digested the information, the voice of the operator comes back and prompts you for the actual telephone number of the place you want to call. Having dialled this, you're then put through as normal.

So how is this going to work with a modem? Let's look at the example of World Telecom.

1. Let's assume your ID number is 40004 and your PIN number 1234. In the UK, World Telecom's freephone number is 0500 626364, which you're dialling from a hotel.

2. In the modem initialization string, enter the usual ATDT preamble followed by a 9 to get an outside line, the World Telecom freephone number, your ID number, your PIN number, and finally the number you want to contact, followed by a hash symbol. In this case let's

assume it's a bulletin board in the USA: 00 1 613 666 6666. The whole thing might look something like this:

ATDT9,0500626364,400041234, 001613666666#

The hash, incidentally, is merely to tell the system that all the relevant information has been entered, and to please get on with dialling. You can leave it out, but then the system takes a little longer to respond if you do.

3. Anyway, firing up the above bypasses the hotel switchboard and connects you to World Telecom. If your modem's loudspeaker is on, you'll hear the voice of the operator asking for the ID and PIN numbers. Then, the comma gives just enough of a pause to allow the system to switch through before the second part of the initialization string – the ID and PIN numbers – are dialled. Similarly, the comma following the ID and PIN numbers gives enough of a pause for the mechanical operator to come back and ask for the international phone number to be dialled. Thereafter, everything should work just as if you'd dialled the number in the normal manner.

I know it looks a little long-winded, but think of the money you'll be saving. Spend it in the bar instead.

Call-back

Call-back services allow people in foreign countries to dial a telephone number which connects them with a call switching system in America. Then that system phones them back and basically 'exports' a US dial tone. In other words, your telephone in the Kyoto hotel rings, you pick up the receiver, and there's a dial tone beeping down the line at you. This can then be used for dialling in the normal manner, voice or data, anywhere in the world. Companies offering this service include MTC, INTEX, Kallback Direct, and STAR*Telecom.

But just a minute, you're saying. I phone the system in the USA, which then phones me back. Don't I then have to pay for two sets of international calls? Yes, that's right.

It isn't as stupid as it sounds, however. In areas such as the Far East, conventional telephone charges can be up to 66% higher than those in the USA or Europe. Add a hotel surcharge to that lot and your credit card might start melting. So by using a call-back service from, say, Japan, where telecommunications charges are extortionately high, you pay for one short (and therefore relatively inexpensive) telephone call to the service provider, and then an international call from them to you at much more reasonable US rates. The savings over direct international connections can be massive.

Of course, this is only going to work if your hotel room can be contacted directly, without having to go through a hotel operator. If it can, then the various services work in much the same way. First, you call the service provider. A recorded operator's voice answers, and prompts you for a PIN number and, if necessary, the telephone number from where you're calling. Then you hang up. A few seconds later, the service calls you back with a dial tone.

Using call-back with a modem is simplicity itself.

1. Configure your communications software such that it's set up for dialling your target number from a direct-connection telephone in the United States. (In other words, pretend you're living in an apartment in New York or San Francisco. If it's a London number you want to call, you'll have to add the United States exit code, 011, plus the 44 for the UK.)

2. To be on the safe side, tell your modem to ignore any dial tone, i.e. add X1.

3. Key the command ATS0=0 into your modem's initialization string. Those are zeros, not capital letters O, by the way. This is the command to tell your modem *not* to

answer the phone. This is important, as I'll explain shortly. Incidentally, just for interest's sake, ATS0=1 says 'answer the telephone after the first ring,' while ATS0=2 says 'answer the telephone after the second ring.'

4. Next, plug the modem and telephone together in tandem using a doubler socket.

5. When the service provider rings in, lift the receiver, fire up your comms package, and put the receiver down.

Do you see the reason for the command ATS0=0 in your initialization string? If it wasn't there, the incoming telephone call would cause your modem to answer the telephone. Modems that do this then expect to be talking to another modem, so they squeal down the line and expect a reciprocal scream from the other end. However, in the case of a call-back service phoning in, all your modem would hear would be a dial tone, which would confuse it terribly and make it refuse to work.

Digital Telephones

One short caveat before we leave the subject of telephones in hotels. Beware the digital variety. These are phones that, as well as the usual buttons, have buttons for such things as the room's air-conditioning, the ice-cube machine, and the television video channels. You're most likely to find them in plush American hotels. If you try unplugging one of these and connecting a modem in its place, the initialization string might well select the hardcore porn channel and reduce your room temperature to $0\,°C$. One person I know of, staying in a Disney resort equipped with such a phone system, managed to set the fire alarm off while attempting a CompuServe connection.

Check to see if there's a data socket on the side of the telephone. If there isn't, you're going to have to either go in through the handset or, if all else fails, use an acoustic coupler. You have been warned.

* * *

And now, we go beyond the realms of the cosy hotel room, out into the real world.

5: In the Office and on the Road

Not everyone is going to be staying in a hotel. You could be trying to log on from an office or a private house or apartment, for example. Here, the same problems regarding accessibility of telephone sockets and so on will apply, although they could be compounded by the vagaries of foreign switchboards, multi-line telephones, or even local customs. Then there are those occasions when you won't have access to a conventional private telephone system at all. You could be in an airport, for instance, or in a busy city centre. Here, it might be necessary to attempt a connection through a public payphone, where one exists. And what if there aren't any call boxes? Then you're faced with the ultimate challenge: wireless connection via cellular modems or even satellite systems.

But before we get that far down the road, let's start with more familiar territory: the office.

Connecting from the Office

In theory, connecting from an office in a foreign country should be straightforward. These days, most hi-tech, computerized establishments, wherever in the world they may be, are geared to the needs of the modem-equipped traveler. If there isn't a separate data socket *per se*, then you should at least find a computer with a modem attached on to which you can transfer your files, or a spare fax socket.

However, on this occasion, let's assume you've drawn the short straw and arrived in one of the far flung outposts of what used to be the British Empire. Let's further assume that this former colonial backwater is somewhat less developed that those in Europe and America. It still regards black and white television and re-runs of the Donny Osmond Show as being state-of-the-art. Finally, the office you're visiting has a correspondingly antediluvian telephone system, of the sort seen in those 1940s private eye movies. How do you proceed?

1. Pretend for a moment that you *are* in a hotel. Are there any visible telephone sockets? If the answer's yes and you have an appropriate adapter, think for a second before you just plug in and fire up your modem. Will the person whose office it is understand what you're doing?

2. If there are no sockets, think twice before attempting a hard-wire connection. Certainly, it might be technically feasible. However, you could be traveling on business and want to make a good first impression. Win a contract, even. Does it look good if the first act of your business relationship is to burrow into your client's wall in order to take apart their telephone system?

3. So before you reach for the crocodile clips, look for a fax machine. Today, even in offices where all the rest of the equipment dates from the days of the Raj, there's every likelihood you'll find a modern fax machine. But pause a minute.

    (i) Is it the only fax machine in the office? If so, plugging your modem in could risk disrupting day to day business. With the owner's consent, however, you could suggest putting a doubler adapter in so that the fax and modem can be used in parallel.

    (ii) Where in the world are you? Think back to the examples in Chapter 2. Is it politically desirable to plug your modem into the fax socket? Could a binary upload to CompuServe result in a sudden kicking down of the door and a visit by the secret police?

4. Sometimes there might very well be telephones and what look like perfectly accessible sockets. Have a close look first, though. Many office phones are of the **multi-line** variety. In other words, there's just one socket, but a number of external lines running from this socket. Each is normally selected by pressing a button on the phone.

Unfortunately, you can't just plug a modem into such a socket, nor can you easily hard-wire. What you're going to have to do here, if possible, is go in through the telephone handset, select the outside line manually by pressing the appropriate button on the telephone, and then dial out as usual with the modem. Will the owner of the office raise any objections to having his telephone taken apart?

In all of the cases relating to connecting from an office, how you proceed is largely down to protocol. In most cases, no-one's going to object. Just be aware that people can get overly sensitive about their telephones and faxes. So if it's no go with either the fax or the phone, it's down to an acoustic coupler.

The Private House

Exactly the same technical problems as connecting from a hotel or office can be experienced in a private house. Just one question you should ask yourself: who's paying the phone bill? If it's your hosts, will they mind you faxing a 100-page document at high-resolution to somewhere on the other side of the world?

In Hospital

I thought I'd throw this one in just for information sake. If you find yourself in traction in a hospital bed, probably the last thing you'll want to do is try to contact an online service through your modem. However, some people are made of far sterner stuff. They see these payphones on trolleys that are wheeled around the wards from bed to bed and plugged into sockets just above the bedhead. 'Aha!' they say. 'That socket looks extremely conventional to me. I will therefore plug my modem into it and contact CompuServe.' And so they try. Unfortunately, the modem responds with an error message. No way will it connect, and no variation on an initialization string will force it to do so.

The problem here is hardware, not software. Telephone sockets in wards in British National Health Service hospitals (though this could be common to hospitals in other countries, too) are wired slightly differently from the normal kind. This is done with the express intention of preventing people from bringing their own telephones in and getting free calls courtesy of the cash-starved Health Service. Actually, there is a way of bypassing this, but I'm not going to tell you what it is because that would make me a party to fraud.

Sorry, but if you do find yourself immobilized in hospital, the only thing you can legally do is attach an acoustic coupler to the payphone.

Payphones

Which takes us to payphones – only to be used if you really *must*, mind you. All the niceties that make public phones vandal, thief, and fraud-proof – no detachable parts, no way of hard-wiring into the main cable, etc – also render them extremely telecommuter hostile. Except for the AT&T variety in some US airport departure lounges, you're not going to find a payphone with a data socket. Which means the only way of connecting is through an acoustic coupler.

I said earlier that acoustic couplers can be very good indeed. True enough, so long as you're operating from a relatively quiet environment such as a hotel bedroom, office, or hospital bed. However, the majority of payphones tend to be in noisy, busy places, like the middle of stations, right under the loud-speakers announcing arrivals and departures, or in the centre of traffic islands. Hardly what you'd call free of ambient noises.

In days goneby, this didn't matter too much because most payphones were of the type that Superman used to change in – all-enclosing cubicles with a heavy, relatively soundproof door. Unfortunately, these are now fast becoming obsolete, worldwide. The modern varieties are open to the elements, with just a perspex covering if you're lucky. This means that ambient noise could pose a problem as could vibration from passing traffic. So if you must use such a telephone, how do you maximize your chances of achieving and maintaining a connection?

1. If possible, try to find one that takes credit cards or phone company charge cards. This will minimize the risk of the 'pips' cutting in and disrupting your connection.

2. It goes without saying that your chosen payphone ought to be in as secluded an area as possible. However, very often you haven't got much choice in the matter. If there's a row of payphones, choose one of those on the end. Setting up in a cubicle in the middle means there's a chance that the chatter of people on each side of you could interfere with transmission, whereas if you're on the end, you've only got one person's cacophony to contend with.

3. As far as is possible, don't choose a busy time of day. It's going to take you a couple of minutes to rig your acoustic coupler, anyway, so if there's a queue of people forming up behind, you will irritate the hell out of them. You might also attract the attention of passing police officers who could mistake your activities for acts of wanton vandalism.

4.   Even if you're using a tone-dial telephone, it's best not to tone-dial through the coupler and handset. Don't ask me why, but in the majority of cases where I've tried, the public telephone simply didn't respond. Maybe they're deliberately set up this way to prevent people using an external tone-dialler and possibly defrauding the phone company. Always manual dial.

5.   Don't place the coupler and handset combination on a hard surface such as the top of the telephone unit. It's usually metallic and will transmit vibrations. Instead, dangle the two in mid air. But prior to doing this, dangle the handset separately. This will eliminate any twists or tangles in the wire.

6.   Assuming you do get a connection, proceed as described in the previous chapter, and hope for the best.

Remember: payphones, especially those out in the street, are for emergency use only. Reliability simply cannot be guaranteed. Having said that, however, I once managed several successful 2400 bps connections from busy payphones in the middle of Florence, with tourists milling around and noisy mopeds scooting past every other second. My efforts were only thwarted one midday, when every single church bell in the city suddenly went off simultaneously.

Public Telephones with Data Sockets

Those of you who make regular trips to the United States will probably have noticed those black AT&T desk and wallphones found in airport terminals and business lounges. Some look like normal telephones; others have small CRT screens built in to display instructions. There are two things that most of them have in common. One: they have a data socket. Two:

despite that, most people have considerable difficulty getting them to work with a modem.

There are a number of reported problems here, most of them caused by the telephones themselves rather than the people who are trying to use them.

1. The data-management part – i.e. the electronics surrounding the phone socket – is handled by a small inbuilt processor whose settings seem especially prone to go askew. This can mean that you can't connect at all, or if you do, the connection speeds are severely restricted.

    Unfortunately, because most people who use these telephones simply place normal voice calls, it's not something that tends to get noticed and reported to the service engineers. So you can find yourself attempting a modem connection and getting nowhere fast. However, as these telephones are usually arranged side by side, it can be a simple matter of moving on down the line until you find one that works. Having done so, report the faulty phone to the relevant authorities for the convenience of the next laptop-equipped user.

2. Many dataphones – as many as 50% in some terminals – have what's called **reversed polarity**. In other words, the red wire is connected where the green one should be, and vice versa. At speeds below 9600 bps, this won't make any appreciable difference and you should still be able to make a successful connection. However, if your modem works much faster than this, you could experience problems. These range from a simple inability to connect up to, in a worst case scenario, your modem blowing up.

    Fortunately, there are devices that can detect this. IBM, for example, markets a little unit about the size of a fat fountain pen, called a **Modem Saver**. This plugs into the suspicious socket and looks out for reversed polarity, as well as checking for overly high voltages and digital lines. Having located such a problem, companies like A R Industries and TeleAdapt sell inexpensive devices called **Modem Cross-Over Adapters** that remedy the situation. As an aside, many new modems are equipped with inbuilt polarity detectors, so this inconvenience should soon be a thing of the past.

3. At many of the busier international airports, there's only a limited number of outside lines. So if you try to dial out, you'll hear a computer-generated 'please wait' message. Sometimes it can take as long as five minutes to get a dial tone, which is usually enough to make most communications packages fail. In these cases, the only sensible thing to do is hang up and wait for a slacker time of day. Or simply not bother.

Connecting Using a Dataphone

OK. So you've found a dataphone that works and whose polarity is the right way round, and that isn't competing with a thousand other telephones for an outside line. With just a few minor adjustments to your software, you should be able to proceed. Nowadays, some 90% or more of AT&T style dataphones will allow you to simply plug your modem in and dial out automatically. However, there's still a small percentage that require the number to be dialled manually. Indeed, on some, the CRT screen carries instructions along the lines of 'Dial out . . . Now engage your comms software' just to make sure you know who's boss.

Anyhow, if you *do* need to dial out manually on one of these telephones, proceed as follows:

1. Disable your modem's dial-tone detection by inserting an X1 in the initialization string. As I mentioned in a previous chapter, most modems by default look out for a

dial tone. If you dial manually and connect, there will no longer be a dial tone.

2. Because you *are* dialing manually, you won't need to put a telephone number into your comms software. Some people just put a comma. However, as I explained earlier, it won't make any difference if the number is left in there.

3. Fire up your comms software and plug the modem into the data jack.

4. Dial the number manually, put the handset to your ear, and wait.

5. When you hear the target number ringing and the first protocol squeal, fire up your comms software and put down the receiver. You must be careful here. If you put down the handset too soon, the telephone will drop the line, just as it would normally. But if you leave it too long, your comms software might miss some of the negotiation protocol being fed to it from the target modem, and time-out the connection.

Now let's look at this using a standard piece of software, in this case, OzCIS, the popular DOS-based offline reader for CompuServe. As with most pieces of comms software, it allows you to create separate session settings for each network or access node you intend to contact. For instance, if you regularly log on from New York, then London, then Dubai, in each of these locations you'll probably want to contact a local CompuServe node. The telephone number will therefore vary, as could modem initialization settings and connect speeds. But you don't want to mess around reconfiguring these each time you check into your New York or Dubai hotel, so you'll save the different settings, to be invoked as and when required.

Anyhow, in Fig. 11 you'll see I've created a host configuration (session setting) specifically for a dataphone. There are only

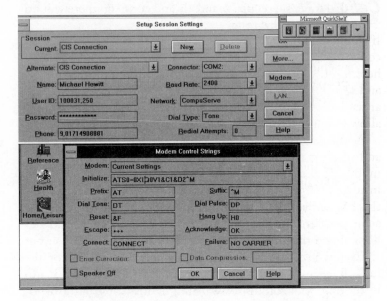

Fig. 11

two changes of note to the normal setup, however. The first is
in the telephone number: there isn't one. Instead, I've simply
inserted a comma, which will make OzCIS wait a second or
so before talking to the remote modem. But, as I've explained,
it wouldn't have mattered if I had the left the number in there.
The second change is to the modem initialization string: I've
put an X1 in there.

And that is that. All in all, dataphones seem to me to be a
nice concept, badly executed – at present, anyway. But as an
increasing number of laptop-equipped travelers start making
use of them, their reliability, and ease of use, should increase
markedly.

But what happens if, not only do you not have a telephone
line in your hotel or apartment, but there aren't any telephones
at all, anywhere in the immediate location? The nightmare
scenario unfolds.

Cellular Communications

If you can't plug into the conventional telephone network, you could try plugging into the cellular network. The problem here, however, isn't just confined to the foibles of reception and transmission. There are also conflicting standards, 'dead' areas, and the fact that some mobile phones simply refuse to allow themselves to be attached to modems.

Actually, if you want to risk it, try this. Connect your laptop and modem to an acoustic coupler, strap the coupler to the mobile phone, and dial out as normal. If the modem is a well insulated model, in more than 50% of cases I've found that this has worked fairly satisfactorily. OK, I haven't been able to achieve speeds much in excess of 300 bps, but I've connected nonetheless and maintained that connection.

Except this isn't recommended – I just think I was really lucky. The experts recommend using either a cellular interface, in the case of analog phones, or a PCMCIA interface in the case of the digital variety. And what might all this mean?

Analog and Digital

Most mobile phones are of the analog variety. Here, the signal level making up either the voice or data stream is continuously modulated. This makes it rather susceptible to interference. Consequently, although a mobile phone connected to a cellular modem can achieve a theoretical upper speed of 9600 bps, in reality, because of the necessity to repeat a corrupt or incomplete data block, you only get about 1200 bps.

Digital phones, on the other hand, convert their data into strings of, for want of a better word, numbers, like CD recordings. Because of this, digital mobile phones tend to be less susceptible to interference than their analog counterparts and can achieve a true 9600 bps. Also, they don't need a modem. Using a suitable interface, they can take the digital data straight from the computer. On the downside, though, at the time of writing, outside of the UK, Finland, and Germany, there aren't any digital phone networks that can handle data.

The digital standard, inasmuch as there is one, is GSM (originally 'Groupe spéciale mobile', but then everyone decided they didn't like French, and so changed it to the somewhat more unwieldy 'Global system for mobile communications'). Currently the network covers much of Europe and some parts of Australasia. The US has a totally different standard, DMS, which is incompatible. Currently, there's only one manufacturer producing GSM dataphones: Nokia. And the phones themselves aren't much use without the computer interface, a rather costly PCMCIA card.

Anyhow, the question is: how good is a mobile phone, analog or digital, for shifting data via a laptop computer? Answer: it depends where you are in the world. The two major UK analog networks, Vodaphone and Cellnet, will only work within the UK. The US network, AMPS, will only work in the USA, and even then can be specific to certain states. Other countries' networks are usually specific to the country supplying them.

The gist of all this is, if you take, say, a Vodaphone mobile phone to places in Africa, you won't be able to do anything with it because there's no network out there to connect to. Likewise, an AMPS phone won't work in London, England. So, basically, what I'm saying is, in the absence of anything like a global standard, if you want to connect your laptop to a mobile phone, you're going to have to either buy or hire a phone that's compatible with the network in the country which you happen to be visiting.

Connecting Up via an Analog Mobile Phone

Discouraging or what? However, let's take the scenario where you're visiting a sheep-farming community in the remote Scottish Highlands and you suddenly feel a need to make a modem connection. Unfortunately, the conventional British Telecom telephone system hasn't extended this far yet.

Therefore, your only chance of making a call is by using your mobile phone and connecting the modem to this.

Now, in terms of physically plugging the units together, there are few problems. Battery-powered cellular interfaces plug into the base of many mobile phones. This interface then plugs into the modem. Unfortunately, such interfaces tend to be relatively expensive, and not all modems are suitable. But theoretically, once everything's connected and the phone switched on, the modem and comms package are meant to behave exactly as if they're connected to a conventional phone line.

Theoretically. It's rarely a case of 'plug in and play', however. For a start, the default modem settings are unlikely to cope with the vagaries of Cellnet and Vodaphone lines. When you hear cellphone users going 'Ya! Charles! Sebastian here!' at the top of their voices in wine bars, it isn't *just* because they're posing. Reception can sometimes be so bad they *have* to shout. So imagine how a modem is going to react to this sort of line quality.

On the subject of modems, it's a good idea to use one that offers something called **MNP10** error correction. This automatically steps the line rate up or down to cope with any interference. It only works, though, if the modem at the other end also has MNP10 implemented. Those that do include the Psion Dacom series and the PCMCIA Pace Microlin Plus models. The modems used by most major bulletin boards and conferencing systems are also MNP10 compliant.

Anyway, let's assume you have all the necessary equipment – a modem, a cellular interface, a cellphone and, of course, a laptop computer – and that everything is now plugged together. The steps are as follows:

1. First, check the reception levels on the mobile phone. Most models have some sort of LCD graphical representation, ranging from one to four bars. Four bars indicates the highest signal strength; one is only really suitable for

voice communication, and even then only if you're prepared to shout down the line and have the person at the
other end continually repeat themselves. For data transfer,
you *must* be showing at least three bars, preferably four.
If not, forget it.

2. Set the speed of your comms software to 9600 bps. You
will not be able to achieve anything faster than this. Or
maybe you will, in which case it might be an idea to contact *The Guinness Book of Records*. Ordinarily, though, at
your first attempt, you may find even 9600 bps is a bit
ambitious, so you might have to re-connect at a slower
speed.

3. Amend the modem initialization string to include:

X1 \A0 S10=30

(i) X1, as you know by now, means ignore the dial tone.
A cellular telephone doesn't produce anything like a
recognizable dial tone.

(ii) \A0 tells the modem to reduce the size of the default
data blocks from 256K to 64K. Excuse me? A normal
modem sends a stream of data of a set size, usually
256K. At the end of this, it says to the target modem
'Did you get that?' If yes, the target modem says, 'All
received OK – please send the next lot of data.' And so
on.

If you use a mobile phone on a regular basis, think
back to the conversations you have over it. Unless it's
a particularly clear line, every so often you'll hear a series of crackles and sputters. These could be anything
from atmospherics to planes getting in the way of the
signal. Whatever, because they tend to cut in so
often, a block of data 256K in size is more likely to
be interrupted by them than a block of data that's
only 64K in size. In other words, it will take more

attempts to successfully shift 256K than it will to shift just 64K. And if a lot of repeat attempts are required, the throughput is reduced correspondingly. That's why you tell the modem to reduce the default data block size to 64K.

(iii) S10=30 also refers to line noise. Very often cellphones will lose the signal for a short while and then, if all is well, pick it up again. If a modem loses the carrier, it just drops the connection and displays the terse message 'NO CARRIER.' Because you're likely to get the occasional hiatus on a cellular line, it's best to allow the modem to give the line the benefit of the doubt before calling it a day. Hence the above code. S10=30 means leave it 30 milliseconds before you panic and disconnect.

4. Once the configuration string is set up, use the comms software to dial out and then await your connection. If all goes well, everything should behave as it normally does, albeit somewhat more slowly.

5. If you're carrying out a file transfer, particularly if it's a big file, always remember to use something like a Z-Modem file transfer protocol. In this way, if the line is dropped – and it's something that very commonly happens with a cellular phone – then you can re-connect and resume the transfer at the exact point at which you were so rudely interrupted.

For what it's worth, in my view cellular modem connections just aren't worth the hassle. As I said, file transfer is highly susceptible to interference, and the slow speeds mean that you're online for a relatively long time. And cellular airtime is not cheap, as anyone who has to pay their own bills will be aware. But in any case, as I said, the cellular networks in many countries won't be compatible with your own. Or there may not be a cellular network in the first place. So now what? Off to The Last Chance Saloon – satellite communication.

Logging on via the Heavens

This is definitely a last resort. Apart from the sheer expense (a typical satellite relay station will set you back in excess of £5000, while the connect charges make prime-time cellphone rates seem extremely reasonable), a so-called portable satellite station is not particularly portable. A typical unit – the Toshiba Inmarsat-C, for example – looks like something you'd perch on your shoulder while playing the latest Reggae album. Even without its peripherals, it weighs more than 10 lbs. Combine that with a laptop and all your usual gear, and you are looking to acquire a serious hernia if you walk more than a few steps.

At the time of writing, two of the commonest portable satellite systems are the Inmarsat-C and Inmarsat-M standards. Both were originally developed as lightweight marine navigation systems. The idea was, you mounted one on your boat with its antenna pointed permanently heavenwards, and were able to get an exact fix on your location, wherever on the world's seas you happened to drift. Also, you got up-to-the-minute meteorological reports. Then land-based versions became available, developed around the same technology and using the same satellites.

There are four Inmarsat-C satellites in geostationary orbit above the equator, called Atlantic Coast West (AOR-W), Atlantic Ocean East (AOR-E), Indian Ocean (IOR), and Pacific Ocean (POR). As you'd expect, their names refer to the regions that they cover. There is, however, a great deal of overlap between the four, such that the UK, for example, has access to AOR-W, AOR-E, and IOR. The satellites are in contact with a dozen or so Earth Stations located throughout the world.

The idea is, you connect your portable computer to the portable relay station, point the relay station's antenna in the direction of the appropriate satellite, and then hit the 'Send' button. Thereupon, your missive travels about 35 000 miles up into the sky, and is then routed by the satellite to an appropriate ground relay station, which sends it on to its intended recipient. Which ground relay station you choose to contact depends largely on where you want the message to go. And while there's no technical reason why you couldn't send a message to, say, London via the Beijing Earth Station, Goonhilly Downs in Cornwall or Blåvand in Denmark would probably be more appropriate.

The *Modus Operandi*

Most portable relay stations work in much the same way. The units usually run either from the mains or, for use in the field, from a rechargeable battery, and are controlled by comms software which is loaded on to the laptop. The satellite station is connected to the computer via the serial port, just like a modem. Indeed, to all intents and purposes, it behaves just as a modem would. Except, of course, you have to point an antenna up into the sky instead of plugging a wire into a phone socket. These days, incidentally, the antennas are usually flat, built into the side of the units.

As the four Inmarsat satellites are in orbit above the equator, the direction in which to point the antenna – either northwards or southwards – will depend on which hemisphere you happen to be in at the time. You place the unit on a relatively level surface, point it vaguely in the direction you think the satellite is likely to be (most come supplied with a compass, so eliminating guesswork), tilt it to some reasonable angle using the adjustable stand at the back, and finally make sure there's no tree or tall building in the way. Then you fire up the comms program.

The first thing that happens is that the satellite station scans the skies for a signal from the satellite. To do this, it has to sift through transmissions from other skyborne objects, like weather satellites, quasars, MTV, and so on. Eventually, assuming it successfully locates its own satellite, it will come back with the message along the lines of 'Slowly adjust the azimuth and elevation of your transceiver until the best signal is found.' In other words: 'Please tilt me until you get decent reception.' The reception values normally go from 1 to 20, the equivalent of the bars on a mobile telephone. The best results are achieved with readings greater than about 10. If you can't manage that, don't bother. Once done, key in the setting.

At this stage, before you can do anything else, you've first of all got to log on to the satellite. Satellites act rather like orbital CompuServe or CIX nodes, in that they don't want just any riff-raff logging on. It's therefore necessary to key in a unique identification number and upload a password before you can start. Then you need to key in a station identifier. As I said, in the UK, there are three Inmarsat satellites orbiting within range, so if you want to talk to Atlantic Coast West, you key in its station identifier, 044; to Atlantic Ocean East, 144; or Indian Ocean, 344.

This done, the software uploads your unique ID number – every satellite station user is assigned one of these – whereupon the satellite tells all the Earth Stations both to expect data from you and that you're ready and willing to receive data from them. If everything has gone to plan, the message 'LOGIN REQUEST IS ACCEPTED' comes up on the laptop's screen. This is followed by a status display, showing signal strength, the current mode, whether you have any messages pending, free memory, and so on, which is thereafter continually updated every five seconds.

Anyhow, because satellite online time is rather expensive, any text you want to send is best prepared offline. Having loaded it into your \send directory, you must save it as a plain ASCII file. Currently, the maximum allowable file size is 32K, which is about 15 or so pages of A4 text. Having done all this, you set up a destination address – usually a telex or fax number, define the comms parameters, and transmit. All these operations are relatively idiot-proof. On-screen prompts guide you through them, while the various commands are accessed via the arrow keys.

Incidentally, in creating a destination address, it's first necessary to tell the satellite in what form the data is going to be traveling; either as text or binary information. Then, for all practical purposes, there are basically three transmit options: telex, for a telex message, of course; PSTN, if you're sending to a fax or a modem; and PSDN if you're going into an **X.25** network. You also enter the name of the recipient, together with the identification number of the Earth Station closest to them which can handle the sort of data you're transmitting. For example, while all Earth Stations can cope with telex messages easily enough, not all can deal with X.25 or, surprisingly, facsimile data.

Anyway, this might sound very long-winded, but it's really just the same as setting up comms parameters – Xon/Xoff, baud rate, data bits, parity, and all the rest – in something like Telix. Optimum transmission speed is currently a rather slow 600 bps, though, should the built-in error correction come into play, this rate might slow down to overcome interference from, say, atmospheric conditions or tightly packed flocks of birds. Incidentally, during transmission you're advised to keep at least one meter away from the antenna because of the dangers of errant microwaves. At just 5 MW cm^{-2}, I'd have thought the chances of getting a cooked head were fairly remote, but better to be safe than sorry.

Assuming the upload is successful, the satellite pings back with a 'received' message, and you know you've done the business. The whole process, right through to receipt of the message at the other end, takes about three minutes, depending on the efficiency of the earth relay station.

Now here's the downer. The process from transmission to receipt doesn't actually take place in real time. What happens is that the data is sent on to the Earth Station and resides there until it's re-routed over conventional telephone lines to its ultimate destination. Store and forward, in other words. Unfortunately this means that you can't log on to systems such as CompuServe, or any that have to precede their data with an ID number and a password. Data can only be transmitted to a modem if the target system's comms software is capable of capturing it as and when contact is established, like with a telex or a fax, which is rather inconvenient. Fortunately there's a way round this, though it's not very elegant.

In the UK, for an initial sign-up fee equivalent to about $16 and a monthly subscription of $8, British Telecom offers a service called the C-Club, which gives members their own personal Earth Station mailbox. Users can transmit their data to these terrestrial mailboxes via the satellite and the intended recipients can then dial in with their modems, log on using an ID and a password, and download the messages. They can also upload messages to the relay station users in the same way. As I understand it, the US telecommunication companies offer a similar service.

After all of that, you may be wondering: why bother? I agree. At the moment, satellite communications systems are unwieldy, expensive, and slow. No doubt in the near future they'll shrink the units such they're not much bigger than normal computer peripherals and no more expensive to use. But it hasn't happened yet.

* * *

So much for all the theory. Before I pass on to Chapter 7 with its brief overview of the various online systems, I thought I'd include a couple of real-life, on-the-road experiences.

6: Real-life Examples

Taming the Telephone in Cuba

I recently borrowed an all-in-one 'Road Warrior TeleKit Pack' from TeleAdapt in order to judge its performance. All that remained was to find some exotic location in which to give it a reasonable run for its money. After some consideration, I gave up on the idea of using it to try to log in from a European capital or the USA – any half-braindead jerk could do that – so a couple of days later I found myself on an Iberia DC-10 bound for Havana, Cuba, from Madrid.

Packed in my suit-bag along with the TeleKit were a Toshiba T4500 486 laptop loaded with Telix and the CompuServe off-line reader, OzCis, together with a Psion Dacom PDF 60M battery-operated portable modem. With V32bis and a reasonable tailwind, I can normally expect a top speed of some 57600 bps out of this lot. From Cuba I thought I was going to be lucky to get 300 bps – if I got anything at all. As far as I could gather, no one else had succeeded, or been idiotic enough to try.

Havana's José Marti Airport was once a prime example of bureaucratic gridlock. Today, however, red-tape is kept to an absolute minimum. The police sergeant at Passport Control simply glanced up, stamped my visa, said 'Welcome to Cuba, Mr Hewitt,' (and even sounded as if he meant it) and that was that. Despite all the highly suspicious computer gear in my case, I was through Immigrations and to the taxi rank in about five minutes flat, which must be something of a world record. I told the cabby to take me to my hotel via the scenic route, through Old Havana and down the Malecón coastal promenade. 'You've got it!' he said and off we sped.

Whereas everyone else's roadside billboards promote Texaco, life insurance, and fat-free yoghurt, Cuba's, like the maxims on the wall of a convent washroom, proclaim nothing but dogma. Driving towards the centre of town you see: 'For everything that we are, we owe the revolution!', 'Long live the revolution,' 'Socialism or death!' and similar. The generic theme is therefore a sort of cheery 'Is everybody happy? – You bet your life we are!'

I had the cab stop in front of a placard of Fidel Castro bearing the words, 'Thanks to what we've already achieved, there's now absolutely no stopping us,' to get a photograph. When I approached and had a close look, I concluded that rather than being an affirmation of any deeply held political conviction, its main aim was to conceal the fact that the building behind had fallen down.

Indeed, at first sight, all of Havana appears to be on the point of collapsing into the Caribbean. Best to call it an example of 'faded grandeur': behind the decaying façade one can just about glimpse traces of the splendor that once was.

The colonial-style Hotel Nacional de Cuba has been completely refurbished to 'international standards,' with several restaurants, a number of well-stocked bars, 24 hour CNN news, and lifts that work. And – most important of all from my point of view – the hotel boasted an American touch-tone telephone in each room which, according to the hotel guide, permitted direct international dialing – sometimes. The only problem, albeit a fairly major league problem, was that they'd hard-wired it into the wall, so there was no visible socket.

According to TeleAdapt's literature, the seasoned international telecommuter laughs in the face of such adversity. I therefore had the customary chuckle before unpacking my kit and setting to. All the items in the Road Warrior TeleKit Pack are stowed in a handy little black bag. Included are: a battery-operated acoustic coupler, a torch, a line-tester; a sharp knife, a screwdriver; several telephone leads, one of which is terminated by a pair of crocodile clips, and finally a bag of assorted national telephone plugs which can cope with 70 countries worldwide. The default plug which connects to your modem is a standard American RJ-11, which in turn connects to the various international plugs.

Because the phone was hard-wired into the wall and its plug seemingly inaccessible, the obvious first course of action was to attempt a connection via the acoustic coupler.

Thanks to all this, you can usually achieve line speeds significantly higher than the 1200 bps maximum offered by conventional couplers. TeleAdapt say 9600 bps is feasible, though when I tested the equipment in the UK I once managed a brief CIX connection at 19 200 bps. Results are of course heavily dependent both on the quality of the telephone receiver and the line itself.

What I didn't fancy doing was trying any international dry-runs, as the hotel was charging $6 per minute for foreign calls. Before I did anything serious, I simply needed to satisfy myself that the coupler was technically capable of dialing out through the switchboard. For this a local call would do. I therefore strapped the device to the telephone, hooked the modem and laptop up, and selected a victim at random from the Havana phone book. Then I went into Telix, set the speed to a modest 2400 bps, keyed ATX1DT and the number, and hit Return.

And I had a result. The modem successfully tone dialled through the receiver, negotiated the switchboard, and a couple of seconds later a Señor Hernandez picked up his telephone and got an earful of Psion Dacom. Oh happy day. So with this triumph I decided straightaway to go for it and dial CIX in the UK. The equipment quite happily obliged, the number rang, the CIX modem squealed at me, and then absolutely nothing happened. It continued to squeal and hiss, but resolutely refused to connect. I tried it a second time and the same thing occurred. And a third time. By now I was $18 down and with nothing to show for it. Time to change tack.

I knew the acoustic coupler worked OK because I'd already used it back home. This meant the problem lay either in the phone line itself or the telephone receiver. If it was the phone line, there would be little I could do about it. But if it was the receiver I could possibly bypass it. This, however, would entail getting directly into the telephone line, necessitating a bit of structural alteration to my hotel bedroom.

As I explained, the telephone wire disappeared into the wall, its actual point of exit concealed behind a heavy wooden sideboard. With a bit of unaccustomed effort I managed to shift this to one side, revealing a plastic plate at around skirting-board level, secured by two screws. With the assistance of my TeleKit's screwdriver I removed this and, using the little pocket torch, peered inside the hole. Not promising. The sight that greeted me looked not unlike the output from a spaghetti factory, so numerous were the wires. Which rather put a dampener on my plans.

What I'd wanted to do was connect to the telephone wires using the TeleKit's crocodile clips. Under normal circumstances, no problem. Unscrew a junction box in the UK, for example, and you'll usually find a maximum of four or five wires. But regardless of the number, in any telephone only two of them are actually connected to the exchange or switchboard. The trick is to identify which two.

To assist here, the TeleKit comes with a TeleTester, a four inch long device terminated by an RJ-11 plug which connects via an adapter to the crocodile clips. If you connect the clips to the wrong pair of wires, nothing happens. If you select the right pair, the TeleTester's diode glows green. If you select the right pair but get them reversed, it glows red. It sounds a bit of a hassle, but with a little practice you can generally identify the correct set within seconds − if there are just five to choose from. However, the prospect of sifting through the seemingly dozens of Cuban wires, all of the same color, was sufficiently daunting to persuade me to replace the plastic plate and try something else.

I mentioned the fact that the Nacional had a fax number and I'd noticed that all the telephone equipment in the hotel was manufactured in the USA. It therefore followed that their fax machine would also be North American in origin, which possibly meant that it would go out through a standard RJ-11 socket. Which meant that if I could get access to that socket with my modem, everything would be OK. Theoretically.

I unfortunately underestimated the extent of a Cuban's emotional bonding to his fax machine. Maybe because there are so few of them in the country, they tend to be selfishly nurtured. When I first asked if I could plug my modem into his fax socket, the hotel employee in question reacted as if I'd said something risqué. But I did eventually find a less hostile employee who studied my proffered RJ-11 for a minute or two and then said, yes, it was technically possible to plug in my modem, but I'd have to do it under the supervision of a telecommunications technician. And where, I asked, might I find such a person? Unfortunately, I was told, there was only one in Havana, and he was away for the moment, presumably assisting at the birth of a Vodaphone. If and when he put in an appearance, I'd be informed.

Anyhow, I waited over a day, but still no technician arrived. At this point impatience overcame me and I decided to have another crack at my telephone wires. What I planned to do was go through the lot with the TeleTester and, by a gradual process of elimination, eventually arrive at a pair which gave me a green light. In anticipation of a long night ahead, I ordered a large meal courtesy of room service, together with a bottle of Johnny Walker Black. Then I unscrewed the wall plate and set to.

In fact – and I think this was more by luck than anything else – it only took ten minutes to identify the correct pair, which was hardly enough time to finish a single scotch. Anyway, I marked the wires for future reference with pieces of tape and then plugged the cable into my modem. At this point I must have tugged at something, because out from the side of the wall popped a little junction box. And in the junction box was the telephone plug – an American RJ-11. I should have looked for something like this from the very beginning and made life a lot easier for myself, but there you go.

This discovery made things slightly neater. Into the RJ-11 I inserted TeleAdapt's US Doubler, a twin-socket adapter which allowed me to connect both the phone and the modem in tandem. This way I was able to check that the line was functioning OK and that my efforts with the TeleTester hadn't dislodged anything vital. Then I got the modem and software to dial the CIX Surbiton number once more. It rang, my Dacom said hello to the CIX Miracom, and vice-versa, and then everything went silent. The modems refused to negotiate a protocol. Why?

Obviously the problem was the quality of the phone line. To gauge how bad it actually was, I phoned a friend in the UK and said hello. She said something completely different, because I'd forgotten Cuba was five hours behind British Summer Time, so for her it was 2.00 am in the morning. Anyhow, our ensuing telephone conversation was punctuated by whistles, echoes, and background conversations in Spanish. We both had to shout to make each other understood. So if we couldn't communicate effectively, there was no way the modems were going to, TeleKit or no. So was this the end?

The really annoying thing was that, according to the staff who operated it, the hotel's fax machine seemed to have no problems. It could have been on a clean data line, I supposed. Then again, at certain times of day, I've often experienced problems faxing abroad to far-flung countries. Maybe it was the same in Cuba. At around 9.00 pm Havana time, all the lines, both local and international, would surely be buzzing with activity, creating a great deal of interference. What if I waited until things calmed down? Accordingly, I took myself and my scotch to the nearby Le Parisien Cabaret, and sat through two and a half hours of awful salsa music.

On my return to the room at 11.40 pm I tried again. ATX1DT8844813901255. It went through the switchboard, dialled, and rang. This time the line sounded a lot cleaner. Then the modems squealed at one another. Finally, after a delay of about ten seconds, I got the CONNECT 2400 message. I was through. After logging in, I uploaded a file, answered a few pending mail messages, saying 'hello from Havana,' and logged off. Then I tried again, this time to CompuServe's London node at the more ambitious speed of 9600 bps. And once again it worked and I uploaded a couple more files. In fact it didn't just work, it worked very well. According to the linespeed rating within OzCis, my throughput was about 75% efficient. Considering the distance and the fact that the Havana exchange must be over 40 years old, I think this compares very favorably with the 96% I usually get in London.

To Viareggio and Florence

At the moment I'm a thousand miles from London, sheltering from the fierce afternoon sun under a canopy of cypress trees in the company of a red-eyed lizard, numerous unidentifiable crawling things, and a curious green and white chirping insect. On my lap is a power-hungry little portable computer, by my side are a couple of bottles of Chianti and a liter of chilled mineral water, while before me in the distance, shimmering in a heat haze, are spread the marvels of Renaissance Florence: the Cathedral of Santa Maria del Fiore, the Ponte Vecchio, and the Palazzo Uffizi, to name but a few.

So what? Very well, you soulless people, I shall get to the point.

Whenever you read any of those glossy magazines produced by – let's choose a fictitious electronic information service – BabbageServe, you'll find they always carry at least one article along the lines of 'Jim di Nuto, Beirut hostage, keeps in touch courtesy of BabbageServe.' In it Jim, with all the zeal of a convert extols the virtues of BabbageServe's international computer network which allows him to keep daily tabs on the Dow Jones and e-mail, despite being shackled to a radiator in a fetid basement.

I've often experienced severe difficulties just getting through to CIX in Surbiton from inner London, and that's *without* handcuffs and a blindfold. So to suggest that it's an utter doddle for the layperson to connect over international lines has always struck me as being grossly misleading. However, this summer I decided to check it out for myself. Accordingly, I acquired the necessary equipment and approached a sympathetic travel agent.

My preferred destination – a payphone-equipped malarial swamp in the middle of nowhere – turned out to be fully booked up. I therefore reluctantly settled for a couple of five star hotels in Italy where at least I'd have functioning telephones. Thus booked, I awaited the said day, then packed my luggage and departed for Heathrow and a flight to Pisa.

I never bother with suitcases; they tend to either wander or get chewed. Besides, circling a luggage carousel like a bunch of expectant fathers in a maternity ward ('Could that be mine? It's got *my* handles . . . .') has always seemed demeaning. So instead I take a suitbag which is generally acceptable as cabin luggage. Generally. Stick a 'portable' computer in there with all its paraphernalia, though, and problems start before you even get on the plane.

Those problems were as follows: Librex T386SX plus two spare nickel-hydride batteries, external floppy drive, mains lead and international adapter; Psion Dacom modem plus penlight batteries; RS-232 lead; Italian telephone adapter; acoustic coupler; UK phone cable; phone cable with a couple of fearsome crocodile clips on the end; set of screwdrivers; masking tape; box of floppy disks; cuddly toy. Try hauling that lot through a security check and *not* setting off every alarm in the airport.

Straightaway a couple of heavies pounced and gave me a thorough frisking. They disembowelled my bag and checked absolutely everything, even to the extent of squeezing my toothpaste (presumably to ensure there was nothing lethal in the stripes). Only when they'd grudgingly concluded that my explosive yield was likely to be minimal was I allowed through to the international departure lounge. Unfortunately further hassle followed in the plane.

The Alitalia cabin crew, normally the most affable of airborne beings, looked thoroughly dismayed as they beheld what I was trying to pass off as hand luggage. Packed full of clothes the suitbag usually stows quite happily in an overhead locker, but stuffed up with all the supplementary gear as well the thing looked to be on the point of giving birth to triplets. So no way, despite much pushing, shoving, and a variety of deleted expletives, would it fit. Consequently I was ordered to slide it beneath my seat, which entailed spending the whole two hour flight in a near foetal position. They wouldn't allow me to take the computer out and fire it up, either, convinced that an injudicious use of [Alt][F10] on my part might interfere with the DC-9's electrics and send us all hurtling into an Alp.

Having been decanted at Pisa, I was then obliged to hump all this lot across town to the central station. With the temperature in the upper 80s (degrees Fahrenheit, that is), my anti-perspirant demanded double-pay. No wonder the city's campanillo was visibly wilting. Not that my encumbrances permitted me to see much of the Leaning Tower, nor any of the other sights for that matter. Once on the Viareggio-bound train, I keyed in a suitably vitriolic essay, laying into so-called portable technology in no uncertain terms.

Viareggio is a sort of Italian Bournemouth; a sleepy seaside town complete with stucco-peeling and *fin de siècle* architecture. At times it seemed the only people under 90 were the 'ladies of easy virtue,' and I'd swear some of *them* needed walking aids. If elephants were indigenous to Italy, I thought, here's where you'd find their graveyard. Nevertheless my hotel was pleasant enough, even though I had to pass through a phalanx of heavily armed bouncers to get to my room. Fortunately, it was equipped with an Italian socket, a three pronged beast looking not unlike one of the old British round-pin AC plugs. I say 'fortunately' because, thanks to my special adapter, I could connect directly instead of having to break out the acoustic coupler.

There was an initial problem with the modem which refused to believe that the triple-beep plus static concerto coming down the line was a proper dial tone. However, once an **X1** – Hayes for 'Ignore this foreign gibberish and dial out regardless' – had been added to the Telix initialization string, I appeared to be in business. I keyed in CompuServe's Zurich number and sat back to await developments.

At first there was an agonizing delay as various national and international telephone exchanges started having meaningful dialogues. Then there was silence for at least 10 seconds. Then, just as I was about to unplug and give up, the holy grail itself, **Connect 2400**, flashed up on my screen. I was in. It had worked first time round, no messing, no sweat. I had become an international telecommuter *par excellence*. I therefore raided the mini-bar and opened half a bottle of sparkling wine to celebrate.

Later on in the downstairs lounge, I settled down to compose a number of messages of self-congratulation for the benefit of colleagues in the UK and elsewhere. The future is here and now, I said. No longer are international travelers constrained by the limits of distance and national borders. Give them a computer and access to a telephone and, like God, they become omnipresent.

Unlike, God, however, they're surcharged to the tune of at least $3 a minute for the privilege of making calls from their hotel bedrooms. So over the next few nights I had to be very careful exactly when I logged on and for how long. At home, my Miracom modem promises, and sometimes even delivers,

38 400 bps. Unfortunately this Psion Dacom modem can only splutter at 2400 bps, making the downloading of things such as .gif image files a very expensive option.

Speed problems became more apparent at my next stop, Florence. On entering my hotel bedroom for the first time I was most irritated to discover that the damn telephone was hardwired into the wall, its modesty protected by several inches of solid oak and brass paneling. The only way to gain direct access to the line would have been to make like a pop star and trash the room. Unfortunately it isn't the sort of hotel a pop star is likely to be staying in – more rococo than rock, with a sprinkling of elderly matrons – so that would have been a difficult ruse to pull off. Anyway, taking a pickaxe to the decor just for the sake of CIX and CompuServe seemed a bit extreme. It was therefore time to take out the acoustic coupler. What I didn't fancy doing, though, was paying hotel rates for what at best was likely to be a 1200 bps connection or, more probably, 300 bps. Time, then, to go public.

Florence is the jewel of the Renaissance world, yet here was I, ignoring the splendors of its art and architecture in favor of a tour of the city's payphones. The locals must have thought I was Clark Kent. What I needed was a phone in a soundproof booth as opposed to a noisy outdoor type. Fortunately I came across one in a little bar just by the Piazza Duomo that seemed to fit the bill. So after a quick beer I spent several embarrassing minutes attempting, in a mixture of bad Italian and sign-language, to explain to the establishment's proprietor exactly what I wanted to do to his telephone and displaying the equipment with which I proposed doing it. Not surprisingly, the man looked slightly worried. To the uninitiated an acoustic coupler must seem like some sort of weird piece of experimental apparatus.

Eventually, though, he acceded to my requests and I was left to myself in the booth. And, once again, it went swimmingly – to a point. When I'd strapped the bits and pieces to the receiver and dialled the number, I was mightily chuffed to get through first time, receiving a cheery 'Connect 1200' from Surbiton. Unfortunately this was soon joined by a plethora of Greek and mathematical symbols, too, which made it look as if I'd got a crossed line with a quantum physicist. Then, to cap it all, every church bell in town started ringing. Not even Z-Modem and MNP5 could survive that. So defeated, I beat a retreat to the comparative tranquillity of my hotel bedroom and tried again.

Back there I followed the rule book to the letter and smothered the receiver/acoustic coupler combination under bedclothes and pillows. The experts say that this *should* provide sufficient soundproofing to give a decent connection. And indeed it did, but only at 1200 bps. All subsequent logons, therefore, have been made this way.

And my conclusions? With the exception of the phone booth débacle, everything worked perfectly – to my great surprise. With the right equipment you really can keep in touch. From Italy, anyway.

Online at 1200 Feet[†]

According to the experts, you've got more chance of creating an impact-resistant blancmange than you have of achieving a consistently reliable modem connection via a mobile phone. Nevertheless, I resolved to try. Doing so in a conventional office environment, however, would have been a bit too easy. Instead, I decided to ascend skywards and log on from a helicopter.

Why anyone would actually want or need to connect by cellphone in the first place, even at sea level, has always puzzled me. Is there *anywhere* in the UK that's so remote it doesn't have at least have *one* unvandalized payphone? (Maybe isolated

---

[†] Since attempting this, I have found it to be illegal. Refer to the end of the chapter for more details.

crofters or sheep farmers have their own Internet newsgroups, and it's the only way they can log on.) Anyhow, TeleAdapt, in Hatch End, loaned me an Axcell cellular interface and an OKI mobile phone. My laptop was an NEC Versa V equipped with a Pace Microlin NB 32 Plus PCMCIA modem.

I was warned it isn't a 'plug in and play' procedure. For a start, the default modem settings aren't supposed to be able to cope with the vagaries of Cellnet and Vodaphone lines. As mentioned in Chapter 5, reception can sometimes be so bad that people have to shout to make themselves heard, so obviously it can be difficult to get modems to handshake, let alone communicate, under these circumstances.

I was advised to use the initialization string: **AT X1 \A0 S10=30 F4**. Translated from the vernacular, this tells the modem: not to (X1) expect a recognizable dial tone; (\A0) reduce the size of the default data blocks from 256K to 64K; (S10=30) if you lose the carrier because of line noise, leave it 30 milliseconds before you panic and disconnect; and (F4) connect at 1200 bps – anything faster is wildly over-ambitious.

The Axcell interface, about the size of an audio cassette, simply plugs into the socket at the base of the mobile. It has a 9 volt battery that amplifies the signals. These go through a cable to an RJ-11 jack which plugs, via an adapter, into the modem. Once everything's connected and the phone switched on, the modem and comms package are meant to behave exactly as if they're connected to a conventional phone line.

And they did. I performed a few test runs on *terra firma*, logging on to both CIX and CompuServe using Telix. The throughput, though of course slower than the 19 200 bps I'm accustomed to, was nonetheless fairly respectable. There were no dropped lines or Greek characters. So I judged it safe to go heavenwards.

Major problem on the day: my helicopter, a twin-seater Robinson R-22, turned out to be somewhat small. With myself and the pilot onboard, it was a bit like trying to share a bidet. Added to this, I couldn't open my laptop. The joystick got in the way. If I'd tried while airborne, it could have sent the two of us into a nose-dive. I was well and truly screwed on that front. Fortunately, secreted about my person were a Psion Series 3a and a 3Fax modem. They'd have to do, instead. I hoped for the best as the helicopter took off and headed northwards, towards Blackpool on England's north-west coast.

When we got within spitting distance of the Ribble Estuary, Blackpool Air Traffic Control buzzed us. Who the hell were we? What did we want? They're understandably cautious. Anyone who wants to shout 'Banzai!' and do a kamikaze dive in that area is almost guaranteed to hit something significant. Within easy flying distance are two nuclear reactors, a nuclear submarine refitting yard, and a variety of military installations. Not to mention Blackpool's Winter Gardens theatre. At a stroke, we could have finished off one of the homes of British seaside entertainment for good.

However, once my pilot had declared our intentions to be benevolent, we were allowed to get in close to Blackpool Tower and circle. At 1200 feet above the Golden Mile (the main tourist attraction in Blackpool, renowned for its amusement arcades and illuminations), I turned on the cellphone and the Series 3a, keyed in the aforementioned initialization string, and said a short prayer.

It might have been nice to report having experienced all sorts of difficulties, and how, through perspicacity, I'd resolved them. In the event, it was completely straightforward. I connected to CIX and got a crisp, clean line – if anything, better than on the ground. So I mailed a computer page with the glad tidings, and posted a message to a conference. Then, for the sheer hell of it, I tried again *without* using the initialization string, at 2400 bps, just relying on the 3Fax defaults. Again I succeeded – possibly the connection was a little more hesitant but it was still reliable

So there you have it. Maybe I was just lucky. But if someone like me who'd never used a cellular interface before can get it right first time, and from a helicopter, there really can't be all

that much to it. Perhaps next time I'll make things more difficult and try it while freefall skydiving.

As mentioned in the footnote at the beginning of this section, since carrying out this experiment I've learned that
using a cellphone at altitude like this is illegal – in the USA
and the UK, anyway – so don't try doing this yourselves. A
law-abiding citizen explains:

'The problem isn't interference with the aircraft systems
(that's a different problem). It's interference with the cellphone system. The cellphone system has a limited number
of frequencies. The same frequencies are used in different
areas (non-adjacent cells), on the assumption that a user on
the ground (on foot or in a car) can't "see" more than one
cell site using any given frequency. When you go up a few
hundred or thousand feet, though, suddenly your cellphone
can see many more cell sites. You can get a very good connection, to be sure, but you tie up the frequency you're using
in *all* the cells you can see, not just the one you're in.'

So be warned.

7: The Service Providers

So, assuming you make a successful connection from your hotel bedroom, foreign office, payphone, or wherever, the next question is: who are you going to contact?

In many cases, you'll be making a simple point to point fax or e-mail connection. However, increasingly, laptop-equipped travelers are making use of national and international commercial online services. Some of these offer e-mail facilities, and very little else. Others are more comprehensive, and include so-called **conferencing systems**, too. Here, you can post messages on a 'virtual' bulletin board, and have them read by other users. At the top end of the scale are those systems that, in addition to e-mail and conferencing, offer reference information on-tap, as well as a host of other resources.

Unfortunately, much of this information is of little use to anyone. Some people might take a certain amount of pleasure in downloading, for example, the full text of *Moby Dick* or *The Complete Works of Shakespeare*, but the majority of us would probably prefer to go to a library or a bookstall for this sort of thing. Certainly, we don't want to pay hotel telephone surcharges for it, on top of everything else.

On the other hand, some of the services offered by the top online systems can be of great practical benefit to travelers. They include online travel agencies, online shops, up-to-date news, stock-market information, and even a pizza delivery service. All accessible from your laptop and the appropriate communications software. In this chapter, I'll look at a few of the more useful services, and who offers them.

The Service Providers: CompuServe

If you want greater detail on everything that CompuServe has to offer, I would heartily recommend buying Roelf Sluman's *CompuServe for Europe* available from International Thomson. This goes into great detail about everything the service has to offer. Here, I'll confine myself to those services that I think are likely to be of most interest to the laptop-equipped traveler.

Founded in 1980, CompuServe is the Burger King of the international computer networks: largely American in flavor, branches in most major cities worldwide, and poised to spread US cultural values to the entire world. In the USA there are over 400 dedicated nodes, while Europe and the Far East have a few dozen scattered hither and thither, with plenty more planned for the near future. Dialling into any one of these nodes connects the user to 40 DEC mainframes based around Columbus, Ohio, which are privy to the thoughts of about 0.025% of the world's population, or just over ten million members. They include business people, journalists, scientists, writers, travelers, ordinary housewives and househusbands and, apparently, Bill Clinton. Send him some foreign policy advice on 75300,3115. He never acknowledged mine, but you might have better luck.

At the time of writing, CompuServe is the only fully comprehensive online service that can be accessed globally. This, in my opinion, makes it the most useful for the international traveler. Currently, anyhow. I know that other service providers are pushing for worldwide coverage, too, this situation will no doubt change before long. Anyway, what has CompuServe got that might interest you in particular?

Travel Services

CompuServe offers the business traveler a host of useful options here. It lists hotels in all the major cities, plus their amenities. If there are any special events going on at your destination, it will give you details on these. And if you want to eat out, the services list the varieties of food poisoning offered by the local restaurants. Then there's details of foreign exchange, including, on occasion, black-market rates. So not only can you find out the going street rate for Cuban Pesos to the dollar, you can even work out how big a wheelbarrow you'll need to carry them all.

Possibly the most useful, however, is the full travel service that allows you to book airline seats and hotels from your own computer terminal and so, effectively, be your own travel agent. Through CompuServe you can access American Airlines' EAASY SABRE, the independent OAG (Official Airlines Guides), and TWA's Travelshopper. All three offer 24 hour price and schedule information for hundreds of airlines and thousands of hotels worldwide. In addition, you can hire a car through more than 50 rental companies. In the case of OAG, it's even possible to book an African safari, complete with hunter and, if required, native bearers. Unlike the back pages of *Time Out*, their listings are updated daily, or even hourly, reflecting availability and the latest discounts. And by using their intuitive menus, you can draw up your own itinerary, bypassing the tour of the cultured pearl factory and the obligatory stop-off at the grappa distillery.

Such services should theoretically be ideal for finding the best bargains on airline seats and hotel rooms. So are the high-street Thomas Cook and the corner bucket shop about to succumb to the technology? Or can they still offer something that CompuServe's virtual agencies can't?

The essential *modus operandi* of the three is much the same, save for the fact that OAG carries a peak rate surcharge of 47 cents per minute, and 17 cents off-peak. Once you've logged on, the system asks: (1) where you're traveling from; (2) your destination; (3) when you're traveling; (4) the number of travelers; and (5) the return date. You can then get more detailed, and specify such things as preferred airline, class of seat, location, and any dietary requirements.

After working on this information for a few seconds, the program presents a list of flights and their prices, highlighting any restrictions that might apply. EAASY SABRE goes further, and offers a 'Bargain Finder' option which, if requested, automatically scans for the lowest cost flights. According to CompuServe, the average transaction, from logging on through to inputting credit card details (all the services charge in US dollars), takes about eight minutes.

Impressive – or is it? In fact, nearly 95% of the people who sign up with EAASY SABRE, OAG, and Travelshopper don't bother using them. Even for those that do, actual bookings, as opposed just to queries, amount to somewhat less than one trip for each registered user per year. The reason is simple: high-street travel agencies can usually offer better deals (see Table 7.1).

'Online services are great tools for *finding* schedules and fares,' one technically aware travel expert explained to me, 'but they usually lack the ability to book the absolutely last available seats on a plane. These are the sorts of seats that airlines tend to pass on to travel agencies and discount shops, who then sell them on at reduced rates.

Table 7.1 *Bargain Flights: Online versus the Bucket Shop*

Destination	EAASY SABRE($)*	Bucket Shop ($)	Difference (%)
New York	468.00	336.00	28
Tel Aviv	520.50	318.00	38
Sydney	1287.00	898.50	30
San Francisco	1683.00	448.50	73
Tokyo	1486.50	862.50	42

Prices (in US dollars) are based on scheduled carriers with confirmed seat availability operating out of Heathrow, exclusive of airport tax. The reservations were made two weeks in advance, with departure specified for June 1, 1995 and return flight on June 15.

'For this reason, EAASY SABRE and Travelshopper are best used as the first step in making a reservation. Then you should pass the information to your agent, who will usually be able to re-book you at a lower fare on the same flight, or else suggest other flights at similar times for less money. In this way, you get the best of both worlds.'

The same is true for hotels. Here, the prices offered by CompuServe's travel services tend always to be the official rates advertised at reception. It's usually better to call the hotel direct and haggle. For example, a single room, mid-week, at the Sheraton Park Tower Hotel in Knightsbridge is given as $322.05 (£215) by EAASY SABRE. Indeed, when the hotel was contacted, this was the rate confirmed by reception. However, when it was suggested that this was maybe a bit steep for just a single room, even though it was convenient for Harrods, the receptionist relented and came up with a lower price. Computers are less amenable to reason, or charm, however.

Basically, you get what you pay for. With a travel agent, you pay for years of specialized training, special deals with airlines and hotels that the ordinary man in the cyberstreet could never hope to clinch, and eight hours a day on the job. But if you want to create your own itinerary, and convenience, rather than price, is the issue, then you may find CompuServe well worth trying.

News Services

It might seem odd to want to download news over your computer if you're staying in a hotel that offers CNN or Sky News as a matter of course, and delivers a daily newspaper along with your breakfast. Then again, you might not be staying in a hotel. Maybe you're in the back of beyond, or in a country where it takes three days for the latest English language papers to arrive. It doesn't matter, though. Either way, if you require access to the most up-to-the minute information,

CompuServe's news services can offer certain advantages over the television, radio and printed variety.

When you enter a news service, you're first presented with a menu of headlines. This means there's no having to scour through pages and pages of broadsheet text to find what you're interested in (anyone who's had to plough through a typical Sunday newspaper will know what I'm talking about). You simply click on those headlines that you think might be worth reading, then they're automatically downloaded to your hard disk for reading at leisure. And when you do come to read the stories, you'll find the information is presented in a far more concise manner than the printed variety. There's no waffle, journalistic padding, or editorial opinion. It's just straight facts.

Another advantage, particularly over newspapers, is the immediacy of the news. It's far more up-to-date. In many cases, you're getting exactly the same wire service newsfeeds as the journalists who put together newspaper and television news, constantly updated by the hour or even by the minute. You therefore get late-breaking stories and newsflashes at the same time as, or even before, they do. So if, for example, a coup or civil insurrection happens to be taking place in the country you're visiting, you'll know exactly when to start running the bath-water.

Anyway, what are likely to be the best sources of news information?

Associated Press Online (GO APO)

This is part of CompuServe's Basic Service, so you won't pay any surcharges for it. Associated Press Online is made up of the same news information that editors use. For convenience, it's divided into such sections as business, national, world, science and health, and entertainment. As you scan the headlines, you'll find that many of them are repeated. This means that a particular story has been updated. The most current version is the one that comes first in the list.

The Business Wire (GO TBW)
This is part of CompuServe's Extended Services, so you'll be paying a small surcharge for it. This doesn't consist of news *per se*, but press releases from various companies, relating to new product announcements, company mergers, hirings and firings, and the rest. Although, in the best tradition of public relations, much of it is pure waffle and hype, The Business Wire can be very useful for those who work in a marketing or sales capacity.

Online Today (GO OLT)
This is CompuServe's own online 'newspaper', and is part of Basic Services. If you're interested in computers and software (someone must be), then Online Today features the day's major technology headlines. These relate to such things as the Internet, new hardware and software announcements, and general techno chit-chat. There's also information about articles in the CompuServe house magazine.

Executive News Service (GO ENS)
The Executive News Service is potentially one of the most useful news services offered by CompuServe – depending on what you do. Put simply, it allows users to file news stories which are of specific interest to them by means of simple keyword searching. In other words, you input a keyword – Sarajevo, for example – and then CompuServe automatically scans all (or a user-selected number of) incoming newsfeeds for that word. When it finds a story that contains it, that story is extracted and placed into a special Sarajevo 'folder,' to be downloaded as and when required. Up to three folders can be created.

Obviously, this service is extremely useful to journalists such as myself, but how might it be so to 'normal' travelers? Well, suppose you're trying to do business in some exotic locale – let's call it Manzanillo – where success is dependent on your anticipating market fluctuations, who's currently 'in' or 'out' in the governing junta, and the state of the country's volatile foreign reserves.

First, create the folder and specify the keywords in the 'Search Criteria' boxes. If you just enter 'Manzanillo', then *every* story that contains that word, however fleeting a reference it is, will be tagged. This could therefore result in a big download. So ENS allows you to be far more specific. As well as entering Manzanillo, enter the name of the country's dictator, General Alonzo, together with the word 'currency'. So the search string is **MANZANILLO + ALONZO + CURRENCY**. Then, only those stories containing those three words will be extracted.

Result: you find that General Alonzo of Manzanillo, with whom you were intending to set up some major arms deal, has been unfortunately ousted from the ruling junta because he's made off with country's entire foreign currency reserve. Conclusion: don't do business with him.

An over-simplified example, I know, but ENS searches are extremely flexible, and can be made using so-called Boolean logic. For instance, enter **COMPUT* + EUROPE – SPAIN** and you'll extract all stories that contain variations on the word-stem 'comput' (* denotes a wild card) plus those that contain a reference to Europe, but exclude those articles that mention Spain. As I said above, there are books available that go into this in much greater detail than I can here, so if you think the Executive News Service might be useful to you, I'd advise you to read them.

Weather (GO WEATHER)

This is part of Basic Services. As its name suggests, it tells you what the weather is, and is going to be. By default, Weather gives you a forecast for the area of the particular CompuServe node into which you're connected. So if you log in from London, you'll automatically get UK weather; from Los Angeles, and you'll the West Coast smog details. If, however, you want to find out what the situation is going to be at your destination, you can select a range of other areas, too. There's even a facility for downloading weather maps.

Faxes and Letters

If your contact isn't on an e-mail system, you can use CompuServe to send either a fax or a standard letter. All this can be done within the normal mail menu. For faxes, you simply put FAX: and then the standard fax number, including, where necessary, exit and international codes, where the e-mail address would normally have gone. For example, **FAX:004471333555**. Thereupon, one of CompuServe's locally based fax machines will process your missive and deliver it, usually within about 20 minutes of transmission. And having done so, it will inform you of the fact. Or if for some reason it couldn't − the remote fax was engaged or out of paper, for instance − it will let you know this, too.

You can send up to 50 000 characters (no graphics or accented characters are permitted), which is about 8000 words, or just under 30 pages of double-spaced A4 text. Rates vary depending on where the fax is going. To the United States, you'll pay $0.75 for the first 1000 characters and $0.25 for each additional 1000. To the Far East, it's $4.40 for the first 1000 characters, and then $0.90 for each subsequent 1000. Even more exotic places, such as Africa, can cost up to $6 per 1000 characters. Bear in mind, if you're going to be using this fax service on anything other than an irregular basis, that fax charges are *in addition to* your normal monthly mail allowance.

If your contact doesn't have a fax machine, no worries: you can use CompuServe to send a letter, wherever in the world he or she happens to be. At the moment, the procedure is somewhat more complicated than e-mail, and requires that you go into the ASCII interface (GO ASCIIMAIL from within WinCIM, or GO MAIL from within other communications packages). Then, having uploaded the message, you're prompted for the recipient's address details. This done, CompuServe will print out your letter, fold it neatly and put it in an envelope, and dispatch it. This done, it will send you a confirmation.

Current rates are $1.15 for each 300 characters sent to destinations within the continental United States, or anything up to $5.50 per 300 for more remote locations. It can be seen, then, that this service isn't exactly cheap.

The Service Providers: America Online

America Online (or AOL, to use the popular acronym) is very much one of the new kids on the block, but it seems to be shaping up very strongly. Since April 1993, for example, it has grown by more than 300%. Some say that within a few years, it may even overtake other, longer established online services. Its main virtue, as far as aficionados are concerned, is its highly pleasing graphical user interface. This is based on GeoWorks software, which looks and behaves remarkably like Windows, but doesn't make the same hardware demands. In other words, you can run America Online's comms software on a simple 286 machine (if you can still find one outside a museum).

One caveat here, however. While CompuServe and others provide 14 400 bps access, the majority of AOL nodes only go up to 9600 bps. Some are still struggling at 2400 bps. This means that all those user-friendly graphics can take a very long time to assemble themselves on your screen. Remember this if you want to dial in from abroad.

In addition, there are – or at least were – two other downsides. First, AOL offers very little real information. It's still primarily an e-mail system. Second, access from outside the USA was either very limited or very expensive. Now, things are changing somewhat.

First, access from abroad. At the time of writing (April 1995), AOL had just begun to expand its services to Europe. By the end of 1995, it should have direct access nodes in the United

Kingdom, Germany, and France. The work is being carried out in association with Bertelsmann AG, a German publishing company. In addition, there are plans afoot to expand the service to Latin America. However, in the absence of such direct nodes, international users usually have to dial in to a local SprintNet node, which still serves as the primary AOLNet backbone. Although this is fairly straightforward, network surcharges can work out to be expensive.

Unfortunately, compared to CompuServe, the variety of quality reference material and peripheral services is sadly lacking. This situation will, of course, improve, but for the moment I can only write about what the current situation is. Anyhow, apart from e-mail, what does America Online offer?

Newsstand

When you consider that in 1993, AOL offered very little in the way of news services, progress to date has been quite impressive. The *San Jose Mercury News* started the ball rolling. Now there are nearly 40 papers online, from *USA Today* to *Road and Track*. It's anticipated that hundreds more will sign up in the near future.

Business Week

Business Week has signed up with AOL. Every Thursday evening you can access the contents of all the domestic and international editions, even before the magazine itself reaches the newsstands. And, if you need that sort of thing, there's a facility for having 'interactive dialogue' with more than 50 *Business Week* editors. So if nothing else, it could liven a boring stay in a hotel. Business people also use the personal finance services to monitor their stock portfolios which on many AOL services are updated every 15 minutes.

The *New York Times*

For those abroad who need their fix and who can't easily get the hard-copy version delivered, the AOL version, which has been available since June 9, 1994, might serve as an acceptable substitute. Unfortunately, it isn't much of a reference work in the true sense. This is because the paper sold the exclusive rights to most of its past articles to the Nexis computerized information service. But what you can get is current news.

The Service Providers: MCI Mail

Contrary to popular belief, MCI Mail in fact offers a lot more than just an e-mail service. However, as it probably is one of the world's foremost messaging systems, I'll look at this option first. In the US and Canada, MCI Mail can be accessed very simply via an 800 number. Abroad, it's necessary to go through surcharged third-party services. But in both cases, once the user's comms software is configured, sending and receiving documents internationally is made as easy and transparent as opening up a word processor file. One phone number and you're in business. Currently, there's an annual subscription of $35. Each message sent starts at 50 cents for a half page, plus 30 cents for each additional half page, although all incoming e-mail is free.

One major, and valid, criticism of MCI Mail used to be its rather austere ASCII user interface, which looked somewhat like CompuServe in the raw, in the days before WinCIM gave it that colorful, graphical look. However, today a number of third party vendors supply software packages to make it more palatable. One such is MailPlus, marketed by the Detroit-based Computer Mail Services. Another is The Wire, from SWFTE International Ltd. Here, the interface looks rather like a Rolodex, with an in-box, out-box, and usual intuitive icons. Any idiot should be able to get it up and running within ten minutes.

MCI Mail: Additional Services

Hard Copy

As I said, MCI Mail offers somewhat more than mail. There's high-quality, hard-copy output, for example. Suppose you're sitting in a hotel bedroom and have taken my advice from an earlier chapter and don't have a portable printer with you. However, the hotel doesn't offer any sort of business service. It's late in the evening and you've got to deliver a proposal for a company board by the next day. You certainly don't want to risk sending them a fax-quality document, but they aren't on MCI Mail. What do you do?

Answer: send your text to MCI in the usual way. They will then print out the document on their own laser printer and, so long as it's received by 11.00 pm EST, will deliver the copy by courier service anywhere within the continental United States. They guarantee delivery by 5.00 pm EST the next day, or before noon in most metropolitan areas. The cost for this is around $9 for the first six pages, plus $3 for each additional three pages. MCI will also courier to over 100 countries world-wide, but of course prices are somewhat higher.

You can also send a normal letter in this way, which can work out a lot faster – if not necessarily cheaper – than sending it by conventional 'snail mail.' Say I want to send a letter to someone in Los Angeles, but I'm based in London. I could entrust my missive to our respective countries' postal services and hope for the best. But even when everything goes to plan, it could still take over a week to cross the Atlantic and then get to the West Coast. However, MCI Mail will actually print the letter in California and mail it from there, so reducing the time lag to no more than two days. Here, the charge is $2 for the first three pages and $1 for each additional three pages.

It needn't just be a plain typewritten document, either. If you use the MCI advanced service, the MCI allows you to register up to 15 graphics with them, including your company letter-heads, scanned images of signatures, and any other fancy logos, for $20 each. You can then choose to add any of these to the letter, such that when it gets to your recipient, it looks much as it would if you'd printed it out in your home office and then signed it.

Faxes
As well as sending a message as e-mail and hard copy, MCI Mail allows you to send it as a fax. Indeed, you can send a single electronic document to as many as 100 Group 3 fax machines simultaneously. There's no problem if the recipient's fax is engaged or out of order, as MCI Mail will keep trying to deliver it for anything up to 30 hours. If it succeeds, it will mail you back to say when the target fax machine finally received your letter. If it fails, it will be equally forthright in conveying the bad news. This is all automatic. Unlike hard copy, however, you can't include any graphics in your faxes. They have to be straight text.

Unlike CompuServe and other providers, faxes can now also be received via MCI Mail. How can this be when, as I mentioned earlier, a facsimile transmission is a bitmap and MCI Mail ASCII-based? In fact, it's a bit of a cheat. A third-party company called PAN FaxMail carries this service out on MCI's behalf. Your contact first faxes their message to PAN FaxMail, and includes your MCI address in their header. PAN FaxMail then scans the document, converts it into ASCII using an OCR reader, and finally delivers the attempt to your mailbox.

I say 'attempt,' because this is exactly what it is. OCR software isn't 100% reliable. PAN FaxMail say their service delivers accuracy of around 99%. However, this depends on the sort of typeface used by whoever's sending the fax. If their document is printed using a monospaced font, such as Courier, and it comes over the line cleanly without any glitches then, yes, you'll get an accurate conversion. However, if their house font is something out of the ordinary, like Bookman Old English or Algerian, or anything that's proportionally spaced, for that matter, then all sorts of weird and wonderful things will turn up in your in-box. The same can happen if their letter included graphics. Be warned.

Dow Jones
As part of their subscription, MCI Mail users are allowed to access Dow Jones News/Retrieval without having to pay the usual Dow Jones annual fee. But bear in mind that the normal Dow Jones connect charges are still in effect. These range from between 12 cents to just under $3 per minute, depending on your access speed and whether you're connecting peak or off peak.

Dow Jones News/Retrieval is probably one of the most widely used business and financial online information systems. There are more than 20 services on offer, including airline schedules, stock market quotes, weather, and business news from the *Wall Street Journal*.

The Service Providers: Prodigy

Prodigy was originally developed as a videotex service by IBM and Sears in the USA, with a colorful, graphic front-end. Currently, membership stands at around the 1 million mark, and growing. Although aimed more at the family and domestic market than other commercial services, Prodigy nonetheless offers a wide variety of bulletin boards, online shopping and, if you're interested in that sort of thing, sports coverage. In due course, there are plans to deliver video-on-demand clips of sports events, using cable television technology.

So much for that. But what does Prodigy offer the traveler abandoned in a hotel room with only a laptop for a friend? Like CompuServe, there's the EAASY SABRE travel service, as well as up-to-the-minute stock market information and consumer reports. Recently, the company included Newsweek InterActive, as part of its ongoing attempt to add yet more reference information. Currently, Internet access via Prodigy is limited to World Wide Web (WWW), newsgroups and, of course, e-mail. No doubt, though, in keeping to the trend set by other commercial services, Prodigy's scope will increase here.

On the downside, Prodigy is only easily accessible within the continental USA. Logging on from abroad requires either an international call or use of a secondary network.

The Service Providers: The Internet

Not a service provider as such, but a service which is provided – if you see what I mean. Getting a direct connection to the Internet is not a problem if you're just based in the one location. However, if you're constantly country-hopping, it will be.

Personally, I've always regarded the Internet in much the same light as my microwave egg poacher: something I really *ought* to use on a regular basis but, because of the sheer hassle of doing so, have never bothered. The 'Information Superhighway' is what its aficionados call it. Actually, it's more of an information B Road, full of potholes and crowded with careless road hogs bearing L Plates. But given the current level of hype surrounding the thing, I suppose it's worth looking at.

Question: what does the Internet offer the laptop-equipped traveler that one of the commercial services, such as CompuServe or America Online, doesn't? Answer: absolutely nothing. Indeed, I'd go further than that. Its sheer uselessness in practical terms is matched only by those multi-function kitchen attachments that claim to be able to blend, separate, and make soufflés, but in the end, can only manage to spray puréed vegetable in your face.

There are three main problems.

1. Unlike, say, CompuServe where you can easily find your way around by means of a system of hierarchical menus, in the Internet, there's no comprehensive list of sites or contents. Information gathering therefore becomes rather like trying to shop mail order without a catalog. True, there are keyword 'search engines' such as **gophers**, but they tend to be rather slow and clumsy. Not something you'd want to waste your time on if you were logging on from a surcharged hotel telephone. So really, to be able to access something, you've got to know where it is in the first place.

2. Although the Internet does offer certain useful services (see below), those same services are usually much more easily accessible via a commercial system. And more useable. How so? Because the Internet is a group of separate, interlinked sites, any overly heavy traffic on one of those sites can result in the whole of the network slowing down. There are documented cases, for example, where sites carrying hardcore pornography have suddenly been besieged by users. Result: a dramatic decrease in overall system performance. So anyone trying to make use of an Internet travel service, for instance, can suddenly find it takes three times as long. And those telephone units are ticking away . . .

3. The majority of businesses only use their Internet accounts for e-mail. Which is probably the best use of the system. Unfortunately, they are normally signed up with an Internet provider local to the town or city where their business is situated. This is no problem for normal day to day usage. However, when they travel abroad, it usually means having to make an international call to access the service provider.

Fact: At the time of writing, there is no such thing as a global Internet service. True, there are Internet providers all over the globe, but each is a separate business, specific to the country in which it's located. *However*, all the major globally accessible commercial online services, like CompuServe and Delphi, offer varying degrees of Internet access (see below). So if you want to contact your local Internet service provider without incurring international telephone charges, it's probably worth signing up with one of them.

CompuServe's Internet Access

At the time of writing, CompuServe had just unveiled its full Internet access. This includes all the usual Internet facilities, such as graphical **WWW** browsers and gophers (see Fig. 12). Which is all well and good, but what does this mean for the laptop-equipped traveler?

Many commercial services, such as The Well on the US west coast or CIX in the UK, as well as being accessible via a

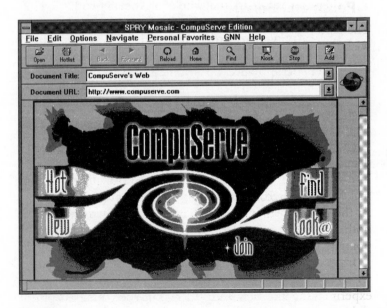

Fig. 12

conventional dial-up line, are also accessible via the Internet using a telnet command. For example, to get into CIX from an Internet provider, anywhere in the world, I would type **telnet cix.compulink.co.uk**. Except, hitherto, as I explained above, there hasn't really been such a thing as a single worldwide Internet provider. You had to set up a special account in each country you were visiting.

Which is where, hopefully, CompuServe, with its established worldwide coverage will come to the fore. If you use an Internet-accessible online service, then CompuServe should now allow you to get to it for just the price of a local phone call, plus the CompuServe charges. There is a caveat here, though. I have tried telnetting from within CompuServe, and although it works, its performance has sometimes reminded me of a snail on Mogadon. It's to be hoped that forthcoming network improvements will speed things up somewhat.

Peripheral Services

The laptop-equipped traveler alone in a hotel bedroom may wish to make use of other peripheral services, either for business or general purposes. So I'll now take a quick look at what I reckon to be a couple of the more useful ones.

Translation

Suppose you're stuck in a foreign country where no-one speaks English, but you've got to somehow communicate business details or whatever to one of the local companies. You could hire a translator, but that can be very expensive, or you could make use of one of the new Internet-based translation services. At the moment, they're all very crude, but they're better than nothing. At the very least, you should be able to get your point across. So what are the pitfalls?

It's said that in the 1960s, the Americans built a super computer to translate English into Russian, and vice versa. As an experiment, a technician fed through the expression, 'Out of sight, out of mind.' The machine whirred for a few seconds (or produced whatever sound 1960s' computers were wont to make) and disgorged the Russian equivalent. This was then returned to the computer to be translated back into English. And the result? 'Invisible idiot,' said the printout.

While the story is probably apocryphal, it does demonstrate the sorts of obstacles computer software has to overcome. Language translation is rarely a simple matter of A = B. Actual meaning can be context related, for example, or masked by idiom. How do you meet both your needs and your grandmother within the same piece of text? *Rencontrer* or *réaliser*? And what would a computer make of 'Let's not beat around the bush?'

An American company called Globalink reckons it's on top of the problem. Recently it announced a machine-based solution which translates text files sent over the Internet. Translations are into French, Spanish, or German, and vice-versa. The fee is 5 cents per word, with a minimum usage charge of $5 per translation. So how good is it?

Globalink covers itself by saying that its system provides so-called 'draft quality.' In other words, if you only need to convey the major points of a message, as opposed to doing a Charles Dickens, the software will oblige. However, users requiring top-quality translations should be prepared to edit the output themselves. 'Just as word processing software doesn't make a person a writer,' says Globalink, 'translation software doesn't make you a translator.'

To maximize accuracy, Globalink offers a few pointers. First – and obviously – the text should be grammatically accurate. Don't use slang or literary terminology. Ideally, sentences should be short, consisting of just one or two clauses. And, if possible, avoid phrasal verbs; i.e. use 'find' instead of 'come across' and 'continue' in place of 'go on.' Finally, if your text includes specialized terminology, invoke Globalink's additional subject specific dictionaries. This is done by including the appropriate abbreviation in the subject line of your message header. For instance, **(com)** switches on the computer dictionary, and **(leg)** the legal dictionary.

The e-mail address for your translation depends on the linguistic flavour required. For English to Spanish, for example, upload to **engspn@glnk.com**. French to English goes via **freeng@glnk.com**. By default, translated documents are automatically returned to the sender. However, if you want to forward them to someone else, you include their e-mail address in the message's subject header.

For the purposes of my test, I composed a simple business letter and copied a short passage of straightforward technical documentation. And, just to show that I wasn't pussyfooting around, I also uploaded some jokes together with the full text of the Gettysburg Address. In all cases, the text went into the foreign language, and then back into English.

And the verdict? A damn sight better than it had any right to be. The simple business letter looked as if it had been tackled by a fairly proficient high-school student. In other words, it had minor errors of construction, but was still quite understandable. The technical translation was adequate, in that terms such as 'LAN' and 'hard disk' were correctly converted. It slipped up on words like workgroup and BUS, however. In the latter case, no distinction was made between the computer and the double-decker variety. The jokes also went rather well, considering. For example, *'Mon chien n'a obtenu aucun nez. Comment est-ce qu'il sent? Terrible'* ('My dog has obtained no nose. As smells he? Terrible.') and *'¿Por qué cruzó el pollo el camino? A conseguir al otro lado?'* ('Why it crossed the chicken the road? To obtain the other side.') But most impressive was the Gettysburg Address. The famous first line became in Spanish *'Fourscore y hace siete años nuestros padres trajeron adelante sobre este continente una nación nueva, concibieron en la libertad y dedicaron a la propuesta que todo de hombres se crean iguales.'* ('Fourscore and seven years ago our parents brought forward on this continent a new nation, conceived in the freedom and devoted to the proposal that all of men are believed equal.') Perhaps not as Lincoln would have said it, but intelligible nonetheless.

Globalink is showing quite respectable results already. In five years, such systems could *really* give human translators a run for their money. They may have to. According to research, the industry average for manual translation is only seven A4 pages per day per person. As the Internet expands and millions more non-English speaking business users log on, machine translation may turn out to be the only way to cope with the glut.

For more information on this, I'd suggest you contact Globalink directly at **info@glnk.com**.

Shopping Online

Why would you want or need to shop online? A good question. But suppose you're on a longish assignment abroad and feel in need of home comforts. Or maybe you're in urgent need of the latest piece of software. Or it could be you just want to thank your host for dinner, and would like to send a thank-you card. Whatever, the emergence of online shopping malls and 'virtual' stores can sometimes make the whole business of shopping more convenient, and faster, than simply popping down in person to the local shopping mall.

The Electronic Mall

CompuServe is the first place to look because, with their Electronic Mall, they actually invented the concept of online shopping. It came onstream in 1985, now has about 150 registered merchants, and is just about the only online shopping service that's actually making any money – so far. There's a heavy bias towards computer and gift items – the sort of goods you don't really need to have sight of before you buy.

Indeed, the very nature of the Electronic Mall probably dictates the type of goods that it can most successfully sell. Despite CompuServe's CIM front-end, the descriptions of the goods on offer are still largely in pure ASCII. There are few graphical representations. While this is no problem when it comes to purchasing, say, Word for Windows or Tom Clancy's latest opus, not many people are going to trust a written description, no matter how witty and informative it may be, when it comes to items such as clothes or soft furnishings; the sort of things you really do need to look at and feel before you buy. Yet for all this, the Electronic Mall has a sizable and ever-growing following, no doubt persuaded by the discounts and relative convenience.

When you click on the Shopping icon in CIM, you're taken through a hierarchical menu structure. You can shop either by merchant or product category. Helpfully, for those who live outside the United States, there's now a separate category for retailers who, for a fee, will ship abroad. And in the very near future, a number of major UK retailers are also joining the CompuServe Mall. Whether this will mean a lowering of their prices to US levels remains to be seen, but it will at least do away with the hassles of import duty and VAT levy that HM Customs routinely inflict on people in the UK who buy through American merchants.

Merchandise includes computers, cameras, electronics equipment, flowers, speciality foods such as smoked salmon and ham – indeed, most of the things you would expect to find in a conventional shopping mall. Having located your desired item, you click on 'Order,' and then either go to the 'Checkout' or continue shopping. At the end, the total damage inflicted is totted up, and you're invited to supply your credit-card details. It's as easy as that. The average time spent during one of these virtual shopping sprees is reckoned to be about 15 minutes, which amounts to a little over $2 in online time, plus telephone line charges (although during weekends, many merchants offer free CompuServe connection). This isn't parti-cularly excessive, though, when you think how much it would cost, in time, money, and sheer frustration, to drive down to your local shopping mall, hunt around with the throng, and make the same purchases.

Shopping on the Internet

At the moment, the virtual tills aren't ringing as loudly as they might. This doesn't mean, however, that there aren't any Internet-based shopping services. There are actually dozens of them, ranging from online supermarkets to vendors of some of the most esoteric objects such as tarot cards and strange herbal teas. Check out http://rare-teas.com/teas/teas.html and see what's on offer. Or if you fancy a used car http://www.dealernet.com will get you into a Seattle used car lot. Or if your purchasing aims are somewhat more ambitious, from the same host, you can buy a house.

But perhaps the ultimate online shopping experience is MCI's new mall, found at http://www.internetmci.com/. Thanks to its high-resolution color graphics and expertly designed layout, this is as near as dammit like shopping from a glossy catalog. Except, of course, that it's interactive. A complete range of goods from major US retailers is on offer, including clothes, jewelry, food, and flowers. As you move from one department to another at the click of a mouse button, logos and color photographs assemble themselves before your very eyes.

Which brings me back to the reason for the subdued tills. If we take the catalog analogy again, shopping online can be like shopping with a catalog where the pages keep sticking as you try to turn them. I was using a modem that sucked data down the line as fast as my Internet provider could supply it, yet I was sometimes waiting up to a minute for each of my colorful department store shop-fronts to assemble itself, likewise when I moved from the shop-front to the graphical representations of the goods on offer. And every minute I sit there navel-gazing is another few coins in the telephone company's coffers. More, of course, if I'm logging on from a hotel.

Fact: the current bandwidth and level of online traffic means that graphics can often be a very slow business. But without snazzy graphics, in my opinion Internet shopping is going to be dead in the water. Hopefully, advances in data compression allied to some sort of speeding up of the network will help sort this problem out. Something has to.

The colorful front-end is also causing another problem, namely, software compatibility. Most online malls use NetScape's server. Since Netscape claims about 70% of the Windows browser market, it would seem that Netscape-equipped merchants would be in a position to process orders from 70% of Internet users. Except that's misleading, because only about 15% of Internet users actually have Windows-based browsers. Which in turn means only about 10% of Internet users can place orders. So until someone develops a true cross-platform front-end, sales will continue to be slack.

And finally, there are those (largely unwarranted) fears over security. People have been wary about inputting credit-card details to the Internet, lest some 14 year-old hacks in and starts living the high-life at their expense. In fact, advances in encryption technology now mean that entrusting your credit-card details to the Internet is about as risky as entrusting them to an ATM machine. Inbuilt encryption software, such as that found in NetScape's servers, mean the chances of someone obtaining financial information fraudulently is maybe one in several million. So you'll be struck by lightning before you get ripped off this way.

* * *

So there we have it. Hopefully within these pages I've shown that using a laptop while on the move, while not exactly problem-free, nevertheless isn't as difficult as some would suggest. Soon, it will get easier still.

Within ten years, I should imagine that every hotel room, airport lounge, and bus station will have dedicated data sockets. Entrepreneurs will most likely be growing rich on a global computer data network, accessible from all parts of the civilized world and a few more places besides, and operating transparently from within Windows 2005 (expected launch date, after debugging, first quarter of 2007). And international

business people scattered hither and thither in different conti-
nents will, no doubt, routinely send themselves memos via
their satellite-linked, Pentium-based, VGA color palmtops.
Tourists and others will send their families colorful electronic
postcards from their Spanish apartments.

But until that happens, keep hold of your telephone adapters
and make sure your acoustic coupler is to hand . . .

Glossary

Acoustic Coupler   A device that clips to the telephone handset to allow modem connection. Generally used when there is no physical means of plugging the modem directly into the telephone line.

AOL   America Online – large US conferencing system and information service provider.

ASCII   American Standard Code for Information Interchange. The most common code for asynchronous data transmission between computers.

ATM   Automatic Teller Machine, found installed outside high-street banks. Commonly known as a cashpoint.

BPS   Bits per second. A 'bit' – short for binary digit – is the smallest unit of information in data processing. BPS refers to the number that can be transmitted over a telephone line by a particular modem, and is therefore an expression of modem throughput. Sometimes referred to as 'baud rate'.

cc:Mail   Lotus e-mail management program.

CIM   CompuServe Information Manager – the standard front-end software for accessing the CompuServe Information service. Available as DOSCIM, for MS-DOS operation, WinCIM, for use under Windows, and MacCIM, for use on a Macintosh computer.

CIX   Compulink Information eXchange: Europe's leading computer conferencing system, based in the UK.

CompuServe   A global online information and conferencing system, based in the USA.

CPS Characters per second. A measure of data throughput between computers.

CRT Cathode Ray Tube. The technology behind the majority of television and desktop computer displays.

DMS American standard for digital mobile phones.

Dongle A hardware 'key' that plugs into a computer's serial port to enable a security protected software package to work. Without the dongle plugged in, the software simply will not operate.

DOS *See* MS-DOS

Doubler adapter A twin socket adapter that allows both a modem and a telephone plug to be connected to the one socket.

DPI Dots per inch. An expression of printer resolution.

DTP Desktop publishing. Page makeup software that allows pages and complete documents to be typeset on a computer screen.

Dual-Scan A type of LCD screen where two separate screens are made to work in tandem to produce a faster refresh rate.

E-mail A service for transmitting computer generated messages between different locations over an intermediate computer network instead of using land-based 'snail mail'.

Excel Microsoft's business spreadsheet program.

GSM Global System for Mobile Communications – the 'universal' standard for digital mobile phones adopted throughout Europe and Australasia.

LAP/M Link access procedure for modems.

Laptop A portable computer, either of notebook or sub-notebook size.

LCD   Liquid Crystal Display. The flat-screen display technology used on most portable computers.

LED   Light Emitting Diode. A semiconductor that emits light when an electric current passes through it. LEDs are commonly used as status indicators on the front of computers and other electrical equipment.

Line Noise   Disruption to modem communication caused by interference on the telephone line.

MacCIM   *See* CIM.

MNP   Mirocom Network Protocol – a common modem error correction system.

Modem   MOD/ulator/DEModulator. A device that turns a computer's digital data into analog data for transmission over the phone line, and converts it back to digital at the other end.

Mouse   A pointing device, used in Windows and Macintosh programs, that allows menus and programs to be accessed by moving a pointer around the screen.

MS-DOS   Microsoft Disk Operating System. The standard operating system for most PCs.

Ni-Cad   Nickel Cadmium. A rechargeable battery technology, commonly used in portable electrical equipment such as telephones and laptop computers.

NiMH   Nickel Metal Hydride. A more advanced rechargeable battery technology which, reputedly, is more efficient than Ni-Cad.

Notebook   An A4 size laptop computer, usually incorporating an internal floppy drive.

OCR   Optical Character Recognition. Software that analyses typewritten or faxed text documents and turns them into

ASCII characters that can then be downloaded into the computer.

Offline reader   A piece of software that automatically logs on to an online system, accesses conference and e-mail messages, and then logs off, allowing the user to read his mail and messages after he has disconnected.

OzCIS   A popular MS-DOS offline reader for CompuServe.

Palmtop   A pocketable computer, usually no more than $6'' \times 4'' \times 1''$, based on electronic calculator technology.

PC card   An alternative, more up-to-date name for PCMCIA cards.

PCMCIA card   Personal Computer Memory and International Association card. Credit card size peripherals, such as memory and modems, that plug into slots in laptop computers.

PDA   Personal Digital Assistants. Commonly used to describe palmtops and other pocket size computers and electronic reference devices.

RAM   Random Access Memory. The volatile memory, within which a computer runs its programs.

RJ-11   The US phone plug standard.

Sub-notebook: A laptop computer smaller than A4, usually with all the features of a notebook, but with an external floppy disk drive.

Telix   A simple terminal based communications package for accessing all online systems.

TFT   Thin Film Transistor. The most modern form of LCD screen technology, providing CRT quality from a wafer-thin display.

Tracker Ball   A pointing device built into a laptop to replace the conventional mouse when selecting menus, etc.

VGA Video Graphics Array. A color display system for computer monitors that provides either 16 colors on screen and a resolution of 640×480, or 256 colors with a resolution of 320×200.

Volatile Memory Computer memory where information is lost whenever the power supply is interrupted.

Word Microsoft's word processing software, available in MS-DOS form or as Word for Windows.

WordStar A once popular MS-DOS based word processing package, now going out of favor.

WimCIM *See* CIM

Windows Microsoft's PC operating system that uses icons and pulldown menus.

WinFax One of the leading computer-based fax packages, from Delrina.

WWW World Wide Web. Hypertext based Internet search software that attempts to impose some order on the chaos that is the Internet.

Index